"This series is a tremendous resource for those understanding of how the gospel is woven the pastors and scholars doing gospel business from all the Scriptures. This is a biblical and theological feast preparing God's people to apply the entire Bible to all of life with heart and mind wholly committed to Christ's priorities."

BRYAN CHAPELL, President Emeritus, Covenant Theological Seminary; Senior Pastor, Grace Presbyterian Church, Peoria, Illinois

"Mark Twain may have smiled when he wrote to a friend, 'I didn't have time to write you a short letter, so I wrote you a long letter.' But the truth of Twain's remark remains serious and universal, because well-reasoned, compact writing requires extra time and extra hard work. And this is what we have in the Crossway Bible study series *Knowing the Bible*. The skilled authors and notable editors provide the contours of each book of the Bible as well as the grand theological themes that bind them together as one Book. Here, in a 12-week format, are carefully wrought studies that will ignite the mind and the heart."

R. KENT HUGHES, Visiting Professor of Practical Theology, Westminster Theological Seminary

"*Knowing the Bible* brings together a gifted team of Bible teachers to produce a high-quality series of study guides. The coordinated focus of these materials is unique: biblical content, provocative questions, systematic theology, practical application, and the gospel story of God's grace presented all the way through Scripture."

PHILIP G. RYKEN, President, Wheaton College

"These *Knowing the Bible* volumes provide a significant and very welcome variation on the general run of inductive Bible studies. This series provides substantial instruction, as well as teaching through the very questions that are asked. *Knowing the Bible* then goes even further by showing how any given text links with the gospel, the whole Bible, and the formation of theology. I heartily endorse this orientation of individual books to the whole Bible and the gospel, and I applaud the demonstration that sound theology was not something invented later by Christians, but is right there in the pages of Scripture."

GRAEME L. GOLDSWORTHY, former lecturer, Moore Theological College; author, *According to Plan, Gospel and Kingdom, The Gospel in Revelation*, and *Gospel and Wisdom*

"What a gift to earnest, Bible-loving, Bible-searching believers! The organization and structure of the Bible study format presented through the *Knowing the Bible* series is so well conceived. Students of the Word are led to understand the content of passages through perceptive, guided questions, and they are given rich insights and application all along the way in the brief but illuminating sections that conclude each study. What potential growth in depth and breadth of understanding these studies offer! One can only pray that vast numbers of believers will discover more of God and the beauty of his Word through these rich studies."

BRUCE A. WARE, Professor of Christian Theology, The Southern Baptist Theological Seminary

KNOWING THE BIBLE

J. I. Packer, Theological Editor
Dane C. Ortlund, Series Editor
Lane T. Dennis, Executive Editor

• • • • • •

Genesis	Psalms	Jonah, Micah, and Nahum	Ephesians
Exodus	Proverbs		Philippians
Leviticus	Ecclesiastes	Haggai, Zechariah, and Malachi	Colossians and Philemon
Numbers	Song of Solomon		
Deuteronomy	Isaiah	Matthew	1–2 Thessalonians
Joshua	Jeremiah	Mark	1–2 Timothy and Titus
Judges	Lamentations, Habakkuk, and Zephaniah	Luke	
Ruth and Esther		John	
1–2 Samuel		Acts	Hebrews
1–2 Kings	Ezekiel	Romans	James
1–2 Chronicles	Daniel	1 Corinthians	1–2 Peter and Jude
Ezra and Nehemiah	Hosea	2 Corinthians	1–3 John
Job	Joel, Amos, and Obadiah	Galatians	Revelation

• • • • • •

J. I. PACKER was the former Board of Governors' Professor of Theology at Regent College (Vancouver, BC). Dr. Packer earned his DPhil at the University of Oxford. He is known and loved worldwide as the author of the best-selling book *Knowing God*, as well as many other titles on theology and the Christian life. He served as the General Editor of the ESV Bible and as the Theological Editor for the *ESV Study Bible*.

LANE T. DENNIS is CEO of Crossway, a not-for-profit publishing ministry. Dr. Dennis earned his PhD from Northwestern University. He is Chair of the ESV Bible Translation Oversight Committee and Executive Editor of the *ESV Study Bible*.

DANE C. ORTLUND (PhD, Wheaton College) serves as senior pastor of Naperville Presbyterian Church in Naperville, Illinois. He is an editor for the Knowing the Bible series and the Short Studies in Biblical Theology series, and is the author of several books, including *Gentle and Lowly: The Heart of Christ for Sinners and Sufferers*.

ECCLESIASTES

A 12-WEEK STUDY

Justin S. Holcomb

:: CROSSWAY®

WHEATON, ILLINOIS

Trade paperback ISBN: 978-1-4335-4853-6
EPub ISBN: 978-1-4335-4856-7
PDF ISBN: 978-1-4335-4854-3
Mobipocket ISBN: 978-1-4335-4855-0

Crossway is a publishing ministry of Good News Publishers.

VP		31	30	29	28	27	26	25	24	23	22	21
17	16	15	14	13	12	11	10	9	8	7	6	5

TABLE OF CONTENTS

▲

Series Preface: J. I. Packer and Lane T. Dennis............................... 6

Week 1:   Overview.. 7

Week 2:   All Is Vanity (1:1–11) 11

Week 3:   Wisdom, Pleasure, and Labor (1:12–2:26) 19

Week 4:   A Time for Everything (3:1–15) 27

Week 5:   More "Vanities" (3:16–4:16).................................. 35

Week 6:   Fear God (5:1–7).. 41

Week 7:   Greed and Contentment (5:8–6:9) 47

Week 8:   The Contrast of Wisdom and Folly (6:10–7:29) 53

Week 9:   In the Hand of God (8:1–9:12) 61

Week 10: Wisdom Is Better Than Folly (9:13–12:7)...................... 69

Week 11: Remember Your Creator (12:8–14)............................ 77

Week 12: Summary and Conclusion 83

SERIES PREFACE

KNOWING THE BIBLE, as the series title indicates, was created to help readers know and understand the meaning, the message, and the God of the Bible. Each volume in the series consists of 12 units that progressively take the reader through a clear, concise study of that book of the Bible. In this way, any given volume can fruitfully be used in a 12-week format either in group study, such as in a church-based context, or in individual study. Of course, these 12 studies could be completed in fewer or more than 12 weeks, as convenient, depending on the context in which they are used.

Each study unit gives an overview of the text at hand before digging into it with a series of questions for reflection or discussion. The unit then concludes by highlighting the gospel of grace in each passage ("Gospel Glimpses"), identifying whole-Bible themes that occur in the passage ("Whole-Bible Connections"), and pinpointing Christian doctrines that are affirmed in the passage ("Theological Soundings").

The final component to each unit is a section for reflecting on personal and practical implications from the passage at hand. The layout provides space for recording responses to the questions proposed, and we think readers need to do this to get the full benefit of the exercise. The series also includes definitions of key words. These definitions are indicated by a note number in the text and are found at the end of each chapter.

Lastly, for help in understanding the Bible in this deeper way, we would urge the reader to use the ESV Bible and the *ESV Study Bible*, which are available online at esv.org. The *Knowing the Bible* series is also available online.

May the Lord greatly bless your study as you seek to know him through knowing his Word.

J. I. Packer
Lane T. Dennis

WEEK 1: OVERVIEW

▲

Getting Acquainted

Ecclesiastes states powerfully and repeatedly that everything is meaningless ("vanity") without a proper focus on God. The book reveals the necessity of fearing God in a fallen and frequently confusing and frustrating world.

People seek lasting significance, but no matter how great their accomplishments, they are unable to achieve the significance they desire. What spoils life, according to Ecclesiastes, is the attempt to get more out of life—out of work, pleasure, money, food, or knowledge—than life itself can provide. This is not fulfilling and leads to weariness, which is why the book begins and ends with the exclamation "All is vanity." This refrain is repeated throughout the entire book.

No matter how wise or rich or successful one may be, one cannot find meaning in life apart from God. In Ecclesiastes, the fact that "all is vanity" should drive all to fear God,[1] whose work endures forever. God does what he will, and all beings and all of creation stand subject to him. Rather than striving in futile attempts to gain meaning on our own terms, what truly is significant is taking pleasure in God and his gifts and being content with what little life has to offer and what God gives. (For further background, see the ESV *Study Bible*, pages 1193–1196; available online at esv.org.)

7

Placing It in the Larger Story

Like the other Wisdom Literature in the Bible, Ecclesiastes is concerned with imparting wisdom and teaching people to fear the Lord. However, Ecclesiastes serves as a balance for the practical wisdom of Proverbs. Although Ecclesiastes finds practical wisdom beneficial, it comes to it along a more reflective path. Where Job asks for personal vindication, Ecclesiastes shares in Job's intensity but its search is for happiness and something that will endure. Ecclesiastes is consistent with the rest of Scripture in its explanation that true wisdom is to fear God even when we cannot see all that God is doing. We can leave it to him to make sense of it all.

Ecclesiastes describes the meaninglessness of living without God. We see that God created the world and called it "good." But despite this original goodness, humanity fell into sin, and all creation was subjected to the curse of God. This brought into the world meaninglessness, violence, and frustration. Graciously, God did not leave his creation to an endless round of meaninglessness. God's response to sin is to redeem, renew, restore, and recreate. The Bible traces this history of salvation[2] from beginning to end. While this process starts immediately after the fall,[3] God's rescue mission culminates in Jesus Christ, who has rescued us from the meaninglessness of the curse that plagues us. Christ rescues us from the vanity of the world by subjecting himself to the same vanity of the world. He who is God chose to subject himself to the conditions of the world under covenant curse in order to rescue the world from the effects of that curse.

Key Verses

"Vanity of vanities, says the Preacher, vanity of vanities! All is vanity" (Eccles. 1:2).

"Vanity of vanities, says the Preacher; all is vanity" (Eccles. 12:8).

"Whatever God does endures forever; nothing can be added to it, nor anything taken from it. God has done it, so that people fear before him" (Eccles. 3:14).

Date and Historical Background

The book of Ecclesiastes is named after its central character, *Qoheleth* (translated "the Preacher" in the ESV). *Qoheleth* is the Hebrew title translated *Ekklēsiastēs* in Greek.

Traditional Jewish and Christian scholarship has often ascribed authorship to Solomon (10th century BC), since the book describes the Preacher as the "son of David, king in Jerusalem" (1:1) and as someone who was surpassingly wise (1:16) and had a very prosperous reign (2:1–9).

Other scholars think it was a writer later than Solomon. The term "son of David" could be used to refer to anyone in the line of David—it is used of Joseph, for example (Matt. 1:20). Also, the language of the book differs in a number of ways from that found in Solomon's other writings. The Hebrew language used in the book is widely believed to indicate a date later than the 10th century BC.

Strictly speaking, the book is anonymous, given that no personal name is attached to it. Since Scripture is silent on the matter, we cannot be confident in identifying the Preacher. In any case, the book claims its wisdom comes ultimately from the "one Shepherd" (12:11), the Lord himself (Gen. 48:15; Pss. 23:1; 28:9; 80:1).

Outline

I. Introduction and Theme (1:1–3)

II. First Catalog of "Vanities" (1:4–2:26)

III. Poem: A Time for Everything (3:1–8)

IV. Fear God, the Sovereign One (3:9–15)

V. Second Catalog of "Vanities" (3:16–4:16)

VI. Fear God, the Holy and Righteous One (5:1–7)

VII. Life "Under the Sun" (5:8–7:24)

VIII. The Heart of the Problem: Sin (7:25–29)

IX. More on Life "Under the Sun" (8:1–12:7)

X. Final Conclusion and Epilogue (12:8–14)

As You Get Started . . .

What is your understanding of how Ecclesiastes helps us understand more fully the whole storyline of the Bible? Do you have an idea of how aspects of the book's message are found elsewhere in the Old Testament and fulfilled in the New Testament?

What is your current understanding of what Ecclesiastes contributes to Christian theology? From your current knowledge of Ecclesiastes, what does this book teach us about God, sin, salvation, Jesus Christ, the church, the gospel, and other doctrines?

What aspects of Ecclesiastes have confused you? Are there any specific questions you hope to resolve through this study?

▶ As You Finish This Unit . . .

Take a few moments now to ask the Lord to bless you, change you, and help you understand and apply the unique aspects of the gospel to your life.

Definitions

[1] **Fear of the Lord** – Fear of the Lord is a godly, wise fear that demonstrates awe and reverence for the all-powerful God (Prov. 1:7).

[2] **History of salvation** – God's unified plan for all of history to accomplish the salvation of his people. He accomplished this salvation plan in the work of Jesus Christ on earth by his life, crucifixion, burial, and resurrection (Eph. 1:10–12). The consummation of God's plan will take place when Jesus Christ comes again to establish the "new heavens and a new earth in which righteousness dwells" (2 Pet. 3:13).

[3] **Fall, the** – Adam and Eve's disobedience of God by eating the fruit from the tree of the knowledge of good and evil, resulting in their loss of innocence and favor with God and the introduction of sin and its effects into the world (Genesis 3; Rom. 5:12–21; 1 Cor. 15:21–22).

Week 2: All Is Vanity

Ecclesiastes 1:1–11

The Place of the Passage

Ecclesiastes begins with "All is vanity" (1:2) and ends with the same declaration (12:8). The Preacher says that everything is meaningless without a proper focus on God. This theme is established and explained in 1:4–11, with verse 4 providing the thesis: "A generation goes, and a generation comes, but the earth remains forever." People are temporary, but the earth is lasting. Ecclesiastes 1:5–7 gives examples of systems or aspects of the earth that demonstrate this truth. Verses 5 and 6 establish two central metaphors[1] that run through the rest of the book: the wind and the sun. They appear throughout the book in the phrases "striving after wind" and "under the sun." These metaphors emphasize two things: the lasting significance of the earth, and humanity's ephemeral nature by comparison.

People would like to do something new, to be remembered for making a significant contribution to the world; they long and strive for lasting significance but cannot attain it (vv. 8–10). Our efforts are like striving after the wind— attempts for immortality that inevitably fail. One cannot catch the wind—it is here one minute and gone the next, just as fleeting as a human lifespan. All that is done "under the sun" suffers the same fate. We labor under the sun, but will never have the significance or impact that it has. No matter how great their accomplishments, humans will not achieve the lasting significance they desire. Ecclesiastes 1:11 drives home this conclusion.

11

The Big Picture

This section of Ecclesiastes declares the vanity of everything and the denial of meaning or satisfaction in life, in and of itself.

Reflection and Discussion

Read through the complete passage for this study, Ecclesiastes 1:1–11. Then review the questions below concerning this section of Ecclesiastes and write your notes on them. (For further background, see the *ESV Study Bible*, pages 1197–1198, or visit esv.org.)

1. Who is the Preacher, and why is he significant?

---

2. In Ecclesiastes 1:2, the Preacher (Hebrew *Qoheleth*) twice employs the phrase "vanity of vanities." The Hebrew term translated here, *hebel*, can refer to vanity, breath, mist, or meaninglessness and is used more than 30 times in Ecclesiastes. What does this phrase picture?

---

3. At the end of verse 2, the Preacher indicates, "All is vanity." Looking at the rest of chapter 1, why would the Preacher make this statement?

---

4. In verse 3 the Preacher asks, "What gain is toil?" This question is repeated in various ways throughout Ecclesiastes (3:9; 5:15; 6:11; 10:11). Why is the Preacher questioning the significance of people's work and asserting the pointlessness of life and creation? Should his pronouncements cause us to despair?

5. Verse 11 says that few people make any significant impact on the course of world history, while most live and die in obscurity. How does verse 11 drive home the point introduced in verse 4 and reinforced throughout these poetic verses?

Read through the following three sections on *Gospel Glimpses*, *Whole-Bible Connections*, and *Theological Soundings*. Then take time to consider the *Personal Implications* these sections may have for you.

Gospel Glimpses

LONGING FOR GRACE. This passage highlights the futility of life and creation that we all feel. Due to the tyranny of time that erodes and replaces all that distinguishes human accomplishment, our work can be summarized as "nothing new" (v. 9) and nothing remembered (v. 11). There is a cyclical, rhythmic element to creation that appears futile. Seasons always change. The streams continue to flow, though the ocean never fills. Generations come and go and repeat the mistakes of the past. Meanwhile, the earth stands still and mocks any idea of progress. The passage evokes a longing for grace[2] and meaning. This blanket observation of the futility of human accomplishment makes the heart long for the stark contrast of Jesus' work for, in, and through us that is new and will be forever remembered. When we come to believe in Jesus—partaking of the new covenant[3] that gives new birth, new life, and a new commandment—we enter into a new workforce. Now what we do matters, as it is done for the sake of the gospel[4] and the glory of God (e.g., Matt. 25:40; 26:10–13). In Christ, our labor is not in vain (Psalm 112; 1 Cor. 15:58).

ULTIMATE AND LASTING SATISFACTION. Ultimate and lasting satisfaction is found only in Christ and in enjoying God's gifts through him (Rev. 22:17). Apart from the mystery of our union with Jesus, even the best gifts of creation will fail us. If we neglect God in our pursuit of joy, everything good in life— e.g., health, possessions, sensual pleasures—slips through our grasp or fails to satisfy. But if we see that what we have is God's provision and give "thanks to God the Father"—ultimately through Christ (Col. 3:17)—for all his gifts, then whatever we receive from him is seen as a gift that brings true joy—joy in God. In Jesus' words, "Blessed are those who hunger and thirst for righteousness, for they shall be satisfied" (Matt. 5:6). Our labor in the Lord has meaning even when it doesn't feel like it: "Be steadfast, immovable, always abounding in the work of the Lord, knowing that in the Lord your labor is not in vain" (1 Cor. 15:58).

Whole-Bible Connections

FUTILITY. Because of Adam and Eve's disobedience in the garden, creation has been placed under the curse of the fall (Rom. 8:20–21). For Adam in particular, the ground he was charged with cultivating would instead produce thorns and thistles (Gen. 3:17–18). This theme of futility can be traced throughout Scripture, as "futility" can characterize nearly anything pursued apart from God. Without God, our thoughts and attitudes are futile (Ps. 94:11; Isa. 16:6; Jer. 48:29–30; Luke 1:51–52; Rom. 1:21; Eph. 4:17–18). Without God, our work is futile (Pss. 39:6; 127:1–2; Hab. 2:13; James 1:11). Without God, our religious activities are futile (1 Kings 18:29; 2 Kings 17:15; Isa. 1:13; 16:12; Jer. 10:5; Acts 5:36–38; Col. 2:20–23). Even *Christian* religious activities can be futile apart from God (John 15:5; 1 Cor. 3:12–15; Titus 3:9; Heb. 4:2; James 1:22–24). Without God, even our very lives are futile (Job 7:6–7; 14:1–2; Pss. 39:4–5; 89:47; Isa. 40:6–7; James 4:14). Ultimately, God wants to deliver us from the futility that pervades our lives (2 Tim. 2:21; 1 Pet. 1:18), and eventually, he will succeed in doing so by bringing his presence to earth as completely as the waters cover the sea (Hab. 2:14). Then, nothing will be done in futility, for nothing will be done apart from God's loving presence in all of glorified human life.

LIFE AS A VAPOR. In Genesis 3, Adam and Eve were subjected to death and decay as a result of the fall. In Genesis 4, their firstborn son, Cain, kills their second-born, Abel. Abel, whose name in Hebrew, *hebel*, is in fact the word for vanity in Ecclesiastes, is born and dies within 6 verses. His life is but a vapor, a breath exhaled on a cold morning. In Genesis 5, the pace picks up and we rapidly meet men who have sons, grow old, and die—vapor after vapor after vapor. Human mortality is established early on in Genesis.

THE DAVIDIC KING. Ecclesiastes begins with the Preacher described as "the son of David, king in Jerusalem." In Genesis 1:28 we learn that humanity was entrusted with the royal task of "subduing" and having "dominion over" all creation. After Adam, our first king, failed in this calling, God promised that a true and better king would come to conquer evil and restore humanity's rule over the earth. To Abraham and Sarah, God promised, "Kings shall come from you" (Gen. 17:6, 16). This promise was narrowed to Judah's line (Gen. 49:10) and eventually to the line of David (2 Sam. 7:12–16). The hope is sustained with the promise of a son who will rule "on the throne of David and over his kingdom" (Isa. 9:6–7). This points forward to the coming of Jesus, the son of David, who is now enthroned "far above all rule and authority" (Eph. 1:20–21) and who "shall reign forever and ever" (Rev. 11:15).

Theological Soundings

HUMAN MORTALITY. In this passage, mortality is decreed by God (see Gen. 3:19; 6:3; Ps. 90:3, 5) and is universal (Eccles. 3:20; 1 Cor. 15:22). Whether we like it or not, death is inevitable (2 Sam. 14:14; Job 30:23; Rom. 6:23) and, because of the fall, it is a judgment from God (Rom. 5:12–19; Heb. 9:27). But, much like futility, death is neither an original nor a permanent feature of human life. Because mortality was ultimately conquered at the cross (1 Cor. 15:51–57), our future dwelling with God will last for eternity (John 11:25–26; 2 Tim. 1:9–10; 1 John 5:11–12; Rev. 22:3–5).

THE REGULARITIES OF GOD'S PROVIDENCE. In Genesis 8:22, God promises Noah, "While the earth remains, seedtime and harvest, cold and heat, summer and winter, day and night, shall not cease." In other words, because of God's promises, we can expect the natural world to exhibit certain regularities. This dependable nature of the created order gives a rational basis for scientific endeavor and experimentation—two parts hydrogen plus one part oxygen always produces water. And, we can plan our daily activities, knowing that the sun will always rise at its divinely appointed time. Thus, while Ecclesiastes describes these regularities as an example of the vanity of existence, they are also examples of God's grace even amid his judgment. Though he subjected creation to futility (Rom. 8:20–22), he still upholds the regularities of nature so that human beings can depend on them, making rational day-to-day existence possible.

THIS AGE AND THE AGE TO COME. In these first eleven verses of Ecclesiastes, we see a picture of what life is like in this present age. This is signaled by the phrase "under the sun." This phrase does not indicate a "secular" point of view, as is often claimed (the Preacher's frequent references to God exclude such an interpretation), but rather refers to the world and to mankind in its current fallen state, much like the New Testament expression "this present age" (1 Tim. 6:17; see also Rom. 8:18; Eph. 6:12; 2 Tim. 4:10). Because the age to come has broken into the present age by the dawning of the new creation in Christ, there is a tension. On the one hand, life is still very much like Ecclesiastes describes it. On the other hand, we have been given new life through the Spirit and thus we await a full removal of the old as we live in the "overlap" of the new.

Personal Implications

Take time to reflect on the implications of Ecclesiastes 1:1–11 for your own life today. Make notes below on the personal implications for your walk with the Lord of the (1) *Gospel Glimpses*, (2) *Whole-Bible Connections*, (3) *Theological Soundings*, and (4) this passage as a whole.

1. Gospel Glimpses

2. Whole-Bible Connections

3. Theological Soundings

4. Ecclesiastes 1:1–11

As You Finish This Unit . . .

Take a moment now to ask for the Lord's blessing and help as you continue in this study of Ecclesiastes. And take a moment also to look back through this unit of study, to reflect on some things that the Lord may be teaching you—and perhaps to highlight and underline these things to review again in the future.

Definitions

[1] **Metaphor** – A figure of speech that draws an analogy between two objects by equating them, even though they are not actually the same thing. An example is Psalm 119:105: "Your word is a lamp to my feet and a light to my path."

[2] **Grace** – Unmerited favor, especially the free gift of salvation that God gives to believers through faith in Jesus Christ.

[3] **Covenant** – A binding agreement between two parties, typically involving a formal statement of their relationship, a list of stipulations and obligations for both parties, a list of witnesses to the agreement, and a list of curses for unfaithfulness and blessings for faithfulness to the agreement. The OT is more properly understood as the old covenant, meaning the agreement established between God and his people prior to the coming of Jesus Christ and the establishment of the new covenant (NT).

[4] **Gospel** – A common translation for a Greek word meaning "good news," that is, the good news of Jesus Christ and the salvation he made possible by his crucifixion, burial, and resurrection.

WEEK 3: WISDOM, PLEASURE, AND LABOR

Ecclesiastes 1:12–2:26

▲

The Preacher now details his quest: "to search out by wisdom all that is done under heaven" (Eccles. 1:13). In this section, the Preacher names three "vanities" he has uncovered. Oddly enough, the first of these is the pursuit of wisdom itself. He writes that "in much wisdom is much vexation" (v. 18). Why? The Preacher realizes that to understand life truly is to understand in greater measure its tragedies and pain. Because he is wise, he knows that "what is crooked cannot be made straight" (v. 15). In his search for understanding, he had indulged in whatever pleasures he wanted: he sought money, sex, and power, and obtained more of each of these than anyone else. Yet when he considered all he possessed and accomplished, he felt empty. This leads the Preacher to reconsider his pursuit of wisdom, but he becomes frustrated. He is reminded that the foolish and the wise suffer the same ultimate fate and will be forgotten. The Preacher then realizes the third vanity: labor. He considers it a tragedy to have worked so hard only to leave his achievements in the hands of one who did not earn them and who may turn out to be foolish. His conclusion is that enjoying life is the answer to such despair. Enjoying life and the results of our work is a gift from God. Pursuing anything for its own sake will only lead to despair.

19

The Big Picture

In Ecclesiastes 1:12–2:26, the Preacher tells us that striving after anything other than God is vanity and cannot satisfy.

Reflection and Discussion

Read through the complete passage for this study, Ecclesiastes 1:12–2:26. Then review the questions below concerning this section of Ecclesiastes and write your notes on them. (For further background, see the *ESV Study Bible*, pages 1198–1199, or visit esv.org.)

1. The Vanity of Wisdom (1:12–18)

In Ecclesiastes 1:12–18 the Preacher describes his quest. What does he seek, and what is the result of his quest?

What does the Preacher mean by saying, "what is crooked cannot be made straight" (1:15)?

In 1:17 the Preacher explains the methodology of his quest by simultaneously examining wisdom and its opposite. In what other passages of the Bible is understanding related to two things in opposition?

In 1:18 the Preacher says, "In much wisdom is much vexation, and he who increases knowledge increases sorrow." In what ways is wisdom a kind of "mixed blessing"?

----

2. The Vanity of Self-Indulgence and the Vanity of Living Wisely (2:1–17)

In 2:1–2, the Preacher describes his quest for pleasure. How did this quest end, according to 2:9–11?

Throughout chapter 2, the Preacher consistently repeats, "All was vanity and a striving after wind," as well as, "There was nothing to be gained under the sun." The Preacher has stated that he will explore wisdom and folly (1:17; 2:3, 12). What are his conclusions about wisdom and folly? How does the Preacher view wisdom and folly within this section, specifically in 2:13–16?

In 2:17, the Preacher says that he "hated life." What does he mean by this statement? How does this form of "hate" differ from that found in Luke 14:26, where Jesus declares, "If anyone comes to me and does not hate his own father and mother and wife and children and brothers and sisters, yes, and even his own life, he cannot be my disciple"?

----

3. The Vanity of Toil (2:18–26)

In Ecclesiastes 2:18–20, the Preacher explains the vanity of toiling. Why does the Preacher feel despair?

Why does the Preacher hate all his toil (2:18)? What might be a way around this hatred, so that we could actually enjoy our toil and life?

The Preacher, at the end of chapter 2, expresses that "there is nothing better for a person than that he should eat and drink and find enjoyment in his toil" (2:24). How is this enjoyment to be viewed? How does the Preacher arrive at this conclusion?

Read through the following three sections on *Gospel Glimpses*, *Whole-Bible Connections*, and *Theological Soundings*. Then take time to consider the *Personal Implications* these sections may have for you.

Gospel Glimpses

UNDER THE SUN AND STRIVING AFTER THE WIND. "I have seen everything done under the sun, and behold, all is vanity and a striving after wind" (1:14). These metaphors emphasize two things: the lasting significance of the earth, and humanity's ephemeral nature in comparison. We desire to have lasting significance, like that of the earth, but cannot attain it. Our efforts are failed attempts to attain this permanence. We cannot catch the wind. We cannot achieve the lasting significance of the sun and its impact; instead, we labor under it. Ecclesiastes was written in order for us to despair in ourselves and depend on our joyous God and his blessed will for our lives. Anything other than dependence on and trust in God is an attempt to grasp the unattainable. The only remedy to the meaninglessness and depression caused by life after the fall is God. In reference to himself, Jesus taught, "Whoever would save his life will lose it, but whoever loses his life for my sake and the gospel's will save it. For what does it profit a man to gain the whole world and forfeit his soul?" (Mark 8:35–36).

HUMBLE KING. This king's self-indulgence reflects the natural inclination of the human heart when unchecked (2:1–11). In contrast, Jesus taught and embodied self-denial and loving service to others (John 13:3–14). Consider Philippians 2:1–11. Despite his equality with God, Christ "emptied" himself of heavenly privileges, taking the form of a servant and humbling himself to the point of death. The lowest point of Christ's humiliation was crucifixion, a violent means of punishing and degrading the lowliest of criminals. Yet God raised Jesus to eventual universal praise. Through the greatest act of humility, Jesus took the punishment for all our vainglorious desires and ungodly pleasures, so that through faith in this gospel (Phil. 1:27) we might clothe ourselves with all humility (Col. 3:12), die to sin, and live to righteousness (1 Pet. 2:24).

HOPE FOR ANXIOUS HEARTS. In this fallen world, many are weighed down with various anxieties, fears, and troubles. In Ecclesiastes 2:23, the Preacher writes, "All his days are full of sorrow, and his work is a vexation. Even in the night his heart does not rest. This also is vanity." The way to fight anxiety is not to forget our problems or increase our self-confidence. Freedom from fear comes through hoping in God and his promises. The cross of Christ shows that God has indeed come to save us. No matter how uncertain our immediate future, we can trust that he is with us, is for us, and will never leave us nor forsake us.

Whole-Bible Connections

TOIL. In Ecclesiastes 2:18–23, the Preacher describes the frustration of work, the vanity of toil. God gave Adam work to accomplish prior to the fall (Gen. 2:15), but part of the punishment of his sin was that it would now become painful toil (3:17–19). Both realities are borne out in the Preacher's experience, as he finds his work to be both satisfying (Eccles. 2:10, 24; 3:22; 5:18–20; 9:9–10) and aggravating (2:18–23; 4:4ff.). Toil is a sign of the curse. But Isaiah points forward to the reversal of the curse as he exults in the future flourishing of the ground, when the "wilderness and the dry land shall be glad; . . . it shall blossom abundantly" (Isa. 35:1–2). The curse over all of creation, and over all of us, will one day be lifted, but only because Jesus became a curse for us (Gal. 3:13).

EATING AND DRINKING. In this passage, the Preacher concludes, "There is nothing better for a person than that he should eat and drink and find enjoyment in his toil" (Eccles. 2:24). In Genesis, we read of the shared meal between Adam and Eve that opened their eyes to nakedness and shame (Gen. 3:6). Because they were eating in disobedience, the meal had disastrous consequences for mankind. Yet God through Christ redeemed our eating and drinking. In the New Testament, we see Jesus directly connecting his eating and drinking with wisdom (Matt. 11:16–19). Then, at the Last Supper, Jesus instituted a shared meal that his disciples would use to commemorate his death and resurrection until he returns (Luke 22:14–20). After his resurrection, Jesus shared a meal with the disciples (Luke 24:30–31) and opened their eyes to the risen Christ in their midst. Finally, in Revelation, we read of a great shared meal—the marriage supper of the Lamb (Rev. 19:6–9). When God's presence fully comes to dwell on the new earth, we shall see provision of food and healing that will last for eternity (22:1–2). Our eating and drinking here and now simply foreshadow a life of eating and drinking in the presence of God that is to come.

Theological Soundings

THE HUMILIATION OF CHRIST. Jesus' life was filled with rejection, loneliness, poverty, persecution, hunger, temptation, suffering, and death. Jesus took to himself a full, complete human nature, including a physical body, to truly represent humanity (Phil 2:6; Heb. 2:17). His humiliation reached its greatest depth when he gave his life on the cross for sinful humanity. The cross stands at the center of human history as God's supreme act of love (1 John 4:10, 17).

HUMANITY'S PURPOSE. God created man and woman and placed them within a garden to be cultivated (Genesis 2), and this shows his original intention for mankind. We were originally created for joy in fellowship with God (Ps. 36:8–9) and for the ability to work under and for God in a meaningful and fulfilling way. Our work was meaningful because it was part of God's plan (Gen. 1:26–28), and had our first parents chosen to be fruitful and multiply, they would have continued to enjoy God's presence in the garden as it grew to fill the earth. In that state, men and women would have been able to glorify

God and enjoy him forever through meaningful cultivation of creation. After the fall (Gen. 3:1–7), we still strive to cultivate creation meaningfully but are continually frustrated in this effort (vv. 16–19). We still strive to have meaningful and enjoyable relationships, but there is strife among us (Genesis 4). Within these limits, we live out our life under the sun, looking forward with hope to a day when we will live fully in the joy of fellowship with God and others, and will participate in cultivating a new creation that will last forever (Revelation 21–22).

Personal Implications

Take time to reflect on the implications of Ecclesiastes 1:12–2:26 for your own life today. Consider what you have learned that might lead you to praise God, repent of sin, and trust in his gracious promises. Make notes below on the personal implications for your walk with the Lord of the (1) *Gospel Glimpses*, (2) *Whole-Bible Connections*, (3) *Theological Soundings*, and (4) this passage as a whole.

1. Gospel Glimpses

2. Whole-Bible Connections

3. Theological Soundings

4. Ecclesiastes 1:12–2:26

As You Finish This Unit . . .

Take a moment now to ask for the Lord's blessing and help as you continue in this study of Ecclesiastes. And take a moment also to look back through this unit of study, to reflect on some things that the Lord may be teaching you—and perhaps to highlight and underline these things to review again in the future

WEEK 4: A TIME FOR EVERYTHING

Ecclesiastes 3:1–15

▲

The Place of the Passage

Ecclesiastes 3 contains a famous poem. The Preacher writes that there is a time for everything: "a time to be born, and a time to die" (3:2). He reminds the reader that there are seasons and proper times for everything on earth. While God has ordered creation in this way, he has also placed a desire for eternity in the heart of each person. The Preacher concludes that the true purpose of this search is for people to discover God, whose works last forever.

The Big Picture

The reality that "all is vanity" should drive people to take refuge in God, whose work endures forever (3:14). The meaninglessness of life summons people to fear God.

> ### Reflection and Discussion

Read through the complete passage for this study, Ecclesiastes 3:1–15. Then review the questions below concerning this section of Ecclesiastes and write your notes on them. (For further background, see the *ESV Study Bible*, pages 1200–1201, or visit esv.org.)

1. Verses 1–8 are a poem often used at funerals and popularized by songs. How do these verses connect with the Preacher's search in the surrounding chapters? What does this poem reveal to the Preacher about God?

----

2. Explain the phrase, "He has made everything beautiful in its time" (3:11). To what theological truth about God revealed in 3:9–15 does this point us? Where else in Scripture do we find this truth?

----

3. The Preacher discovers that, although God "has put eternity"[1] into our hearts, we "cannot find out what God has done from the beginning to the end" (3:11). What is meant by God's putting "eternity into man's heart"? What is the Preacher's reaction to this truth, and what does he encourage people to think, do, and feel about God?

----

4. What kind of hope do we gain by knowing that "whatever God does endures forever" (3:14)?

_____

_____

_____

_____

_____

_____

_____

_____

5. In 3:14, the Preacher expresses the enduring nature of God's work. He also says, "God has done it, so that people fear before him." Where else in the Bible do we see examples of the fear of God? How does this "fear," stemming from the absolute sovereignty[2] of God and his purposes, cause people to behave?

_____

_____

_____

_____

_____

_____

_____

Read through the following three sections on _Gospel Glimpses_, _Whole-Bible Connections_, and _Theological Soundings_. Then take time to consider the _Personal Implications_ these sections may have for you.

▶ Gospel Glimpses

GOD MADE EVERYTHING BEAUTIFUL. God, not us, is the one who ultimately makes things beautiful (3:11). While this can bring despair, it can bring relief as well. It is not up to us—it is all about God's grace. We are _his_ workmanship (Eph. 2:10; see Phil. 1:6). Our toil belongs ultimately to God's time, not our own—his work is that which ultimately matters and, by extension, that in which he allows us to participate. Within this participation, we are able to create beautiful cultural products, but those works of art and ingenuity should serve as pointers to a beauty transcending culture. Because we are made in the image of a beautiful God who creates beautiful things, we too are able to create beautiful things in our own creaturely way.

A TIME FOR EVERYTHING. Ecclesiastes 3:1–15 lists various times and seasons in pairs. This is the rhythm of human life that Jesus experienced in his incarnation.[3] In one particular example, regarding Lazarus's death (John 11), Jesus delays his response for two days so that Lazarus's death might find its "time" and might then be the means of Christ's glorification before his disciples. Yet in the wake of this planned tardiness comes a torrent of grief and loss so palpable that Jesus himself is swept up in it. He has summoned Mary, and so she comes, along with all those who loved Lazarus and now mourn his loss. We are twice told that Jesus, though strong and sure, is deeply moved in his spirit. He is troubled and undone. He comes face to face with death in all its finality and grief.

Other times and seasons are there in this episode also: mourning time, binding of bandages time, saying farewell time, embracing time, and casting of stones time, as the great stone seals the tomb of a man dead for four days. Always triumphant and so incredibly strong and sure of his own faculties, we see the Lord Jesus himself in his weeping time. In every time and season under heaven, there he is. In order to enter fully into our human condition, Christ had to experience all the times and seasons we do, and that meant enduring a time of sadness and loss.

But most of all, given our fears and our needs, Jesus is there in our times and seasons of loss, thirst, hunger, death, mourning—even in the nighttime when the mind races, as the Preacher observes (Eccles. 2:23). He is not too late, as Mary and Martha presume. He is right on time. His time and season have arrived. And they have our names on them. In Jesus' ministry we see God seeking out those parts of us that find it hard to hear, difficult to accept, and the parts that draw back out of sin or despair or fear. But in Christ, God comes near and understands, and, in the Holy Spirit, God is here and is calling for us.

> ## Whole-Bible Connections

NOT WORRYING ABOUT TOMORROW. The emphasis in this passage on the sure foundation of God's work is connected to the biblical theme of not worrying about tomorrow (Matt. 6:34; James 4:13–15). God works all things together for good (Rom. 8:28), including our own good works (Eph. 2:10), and his word will not return to him empty (Isa. 55:11; see Eccles. 3:14). God works in us "to will and to work for his good pleasure" (Phil. 2:13; see 1:6), enabling us to do everything in good season, as echoed in Paul's command to "rejoice with those who rejoice, weep with those who weep" (Rom. 12:15).

GOD'S TIMING. While God's timing is not always ours, it is always best and sufficient for all that must occur in this fallen world. We are not necessarily faithless or cursed because of the suffering we face in this life. While it is true that we will face difficulties because of the curse (Gen. 3:16–19), we can face it all with the understanding that the God of grace will time all things as he knows best. As we read through the Old Testament, we can see that what might have seemed like forgetfulness on God's part was really part of a grand preparation. Jesus would also come in the "fullness of time" (Gal. 4:4–5) to fulfill God's perfectly timed plan of salvation (Mark 1:15; John 7:30; 13:1; see Rom. 5:6). For Christians, the purpose of *time* is to be "conformed to the image of his Son" (Rom. 8:29). Such conformity rejoices even in sufferings, knowing that all the moments of our lives "work together" for our good (v. 28). Even now, we look forward to Christ's return, coming at a time that no one knows. But we *are* told something of the time (Rev. 19:11–21) and can look forward to his glorious appearing.

Theological Soundings

DIVINE SOVEREIGNTY. God is always personally involved with his creation in sustaining and preserving it, acting within it to bring about his perfect goals. Everything that takes place is under God's control. He "works all things according to the counsel of his will" (Eph. 1:11). His providential dominion is over all things (Prov. 16:9; 19:21; James 4:13–15), including kings and kingdoms (Prov. 21:1; Dan. 4:25) and the exact times and places in which people live (Acts 17:26). In Acts 4:23–31, God's sovereignty, even in predetermining the crucifixion (4:24, 27–28), encourages prayer and confidence (4:29–30). Since Jesus reigns supreme, he is the one to approach with our needs.

CREATURES IN TIME. As physical beings, we are unable to escape the limits of time. Time came into existence on the first day of creation when God separated periods of darkness and light and gave them each names (Gen. 1:3–5). Man was created and placed within the boundaries of time, not as a punishment but as an act of common grace to accompany his creaturely reality. It is only because of the fall into sin that time now works against us, counting down the moments until our death. But in the new heavens and the new earth, time will return to being simply a gracious gift we can put to use for our enjoyment. Because we are time-bound creatures, we can make music (Gen. 4:21–22) and dance (Eccles. 3:4), and in the new heavens and new earth we will continue to do both to God's glory and for our good.

> ## Personal Implications

Take time to reflect on the implications of Ecclesiastes 3:1–15 for your own life today. Consider what you have learned that might lead you to praise God, repent of sin, and trust in his gracious promises. Make notes below on the personal implications for your walk with the Lord of the (1) *Gospel Glimpses*, (2) *Whole-Bible Connections*, (3) *Theological Soundings*, and (4) this passage as a whole.

1. Gospel Glimpses

2. Whole-Bible Connections

3. Theological Soundings

4. Ecclesiastes 3:1–15

As You Finish This Unit . . .

Take a moment now to ask for the Lord's blessing and help as you continue in this study of Ecclesiastes. And take a moment also to look back through this unit of study, to reflect on some things that the Lord may be teaching you—and perhaps to highlight and underline these things to review again in the future

Definitions

[1] **Eternity** – An endless span of time. For humans, eternity has a beginning (the moment of birth) but no end. With God, however, eternity has neither beginning nor end, for he has always existed.

[2] **Sovereignty** – Supreme and independent power and authority. Sovereignty over all things is a distinctive attribute of God (1 Tim. 6:15–16). He directs all things to carry out his purposes (Rom. 8:28–29).

[3] **Incarnation** – Literally "(becoming) in flesh," it refers to God becoming a human being in the person of Jesus of Nazareth.

WEEK 5: MORE "VANITIES"

Ecclesiastes 3:16–4:16

▲

The Preacher believes in divine justice but sees it contradicted, so, rather than working out a smooth intellectual solution or rejecting the principle of divine justice, he throws up his hands in frustration and calls what he sees "vanity." Then he urges us to open ourselves to whatever good things the moment offers as a gift from God. The Preacher is troubled by the way people are divided by their striving. He says that those with power will always use it to oppress; that people are motivated by envy of their neighbors; and that the greedy do not realize how their desires isolate them. In contrast to these examples of individualism run rampant, the Preacher reminds the reader that "two are better than one" (4:9) because people working together not only accomplish a great deal (the goal of the greedy and the powerful) but they also take care of one another (as neighbors should). The Preacher ends this section by writing about a poor, wise man who rose to become king but was forgotten by future generations. The Preacher considers this also to be vanity, for all things built by humans will fade.

The Big Picture

The injustice of the world is a powerful reminder that all people are bent toward their own desires and goals, thinking of nothing besides their own gain.

Reflection and Discussion

Read through the complete passage for this study, Ecclesiastes 3:16–4:16. Then review the questions below concerning this section of Ecclesiastes and write your notes on them. (For further background, see the *ESV Study Bible*, pages 1200–1201, or visit esv.org.)

1. In a fallen world, people experience injustice and wickedness at the hand of others (3:16). How does verse 17 make this reality tolerable? What other passages in Scripture teach that the wicked and the unjust will one day experience God's ultimate justice?

2. According to 3:19–22, how are humans like the beasts?

3. In 4:4–6 the Preacher says that "the fool folds his hands and eats his own flesh" (v. 5) and a "handful of quietness" is better "than two hands full of toil and a striving after wind" (v. 6). How does the Preacher view work and toil in

these verses? What does the Preacher believe wise people should do in terms of work and toil (4:9)?

....

....

....

....

....

....

....

....

4. In 4:12 the Preacher says, "Though a man might prevail against one who is alone, two will withstand him—a threefold cord is not quickly broken." In the context of this passage, what does the threefold cord represent? What does 4:7–12 teach us about community?

....

....

....

....

....

....

....

....

Read through the following three sections on *Gospel Glimpses*, *Whole-Bible Connections*, and *Theological Soundings*. Then take time to consider the *Personal Implications* these sections may have for you.

Gospel Glimpses

THE GOOD NEWS OF JUSTICE. Ecclesiastes contains passages despairing over injustice (1:15; 3:16; 4:1–3; 5:8; 7:15–18; 8:14; 9:11), reminding us that this world will not provide all that is needed to satisfy, correct, or justify. God must ultimately be the one to vindicate the righteous as well as punish the guilty, because we cannot finally depend on the justice of earthly judgments. As Jesus entrusted himself "to him who judges justly," so we must "follow in his steps" (1 Pet. 2:19–23), longing for the day "when his glory is revealed"

(1 Pet. 4:13) and, as the final judge, he will right every wrong (e.g., John 5:22; 1 Cor. 4:4–5; 1 Pet. 4:5).

GRACE OF COMMUNITY. Ecclesiastes 4:9–12 reminds us that God saves us by his grace and brings us into community because of our need for relationships in a world where no earthly relationships are sure. Our Savior willingly identified with us in the loneliness of his passion—he was forsaken by Israel, the Twelve, and even, in some inexplicable way, by the Father—"My God, my God, why have you forsaken me?" (Matt. 27:46). This also highlights for us the preciousness of the Savior's promise never to leave nor forsake us (Heb. 13:5).

Whole-Bible Connections

HUMANITY FROM DUST. In Genesis 2:7 we read of God's shaping man from the dust and breathing life into him. This highlights humanity as a product of both the earth their home and God their creator. We have come from the dust, and to the dust we will one day return (Gen. 3:19; Eccles. 3:20; 12:7). Dust is used also as a picture of the blessing of God, as he promised Abraham that his descendants would be as numerous as the dust of the earth (Gen. 13:16). He repeats this promise to Jacob (Gen. 28:14), later confirmed by Balaam (Num. 23:10). At the apex of Israel's period as a national power, Solomon sees the people of God as numerous as the dust of the earth (2 Chron. 1:9). Yet, a people as numerous as the dust of the earth is *still* going to return to the dust. We need a way not to be bound to the dust, and in the New Testament Paul explains that our union with Christ unites us to a man who comes from heaven to take on our dust and redeem it (1 Cor. 15:47–49).

GOD'S HEART FOR THOSE SUFFERING INJUSTICE. Amid injustice, it is important to remember that God cares for the suffering. God's heart has always been with the afflicted. When Israel was enslaved in Egypt, God heard their cries, saw their affliction, and knew their suffering (Ex. 3:7). He was involved. After redeeming Israel from Egypt, he gave them the Law,[1] replete with instructions to protect the poor, the outsiders, and orphans and widows (Deut. 10:18–19; 15:7–11). Of course, God's suffering servants have always been sinners as well. God's people often went after idols, forsaking him and enslaving themselves to gods that could not deliver them (Isa. 45:20; Jer. 2:13). Christ is the obedient Servant who suffered without any sin. He walked in obedience to the Father but still suffered greatly, allowing him to identify with both the Father in his perfection and us in our weakness and pain (Heb. 4:15). This allows Jesus to be the unique mediator[2] between God and humanity.

▶ Theological Soundings

BIBLICAL ANTHROPOLOGY. When we read about the creation of man (Gen. 2:7), we see man as a combination of a material part tied to the earth (body) and an immaterial part tied to God (spirit). We are the dust of the ground yet also the breath of God. This is the tension of our reality as created images of an uncreated God (Gen. 1:26–28). After the fall (Genesis 3), apart from God's intervention we would be merely animated dust that would one day return to the earth. Yet God has been continuously at work to redeem his "beloved dust," sending his Son to take on our dusty form. Because of this, we will one day receive a body that will be unbound to the dust and incorruptible in both body and spirit (1 Cor. 15:42–49).

THE RIGHTEOUSNESS OF GOD AND VINDICATION OF THE OPPRESSED. In his righteousness, God vindicates his people (Pss. 4:2–3; 7:9; 9:4; 35:24; 103:6; Isa. 50:8; Mic. 7:9; Rom. 8:33). This shows his faithfulness to them (Neh. 9:8; Zeph. 3:5; Zech. 8:8) and his justice (Jer. 11:20; 2 Tim. 4:8). God's righteousness is clearly seen in his judgments (Ps. 7:11; Mal. 3:5; Rom. 2:2, 5) and contrasts sharply with human unrighteousness (Rom. 3:5ff.). God's righteousness shows a true pattern for how we are to live (1 John 2:29; 3:7–12); his righteousness is worthy of our praise (Isa. 24:15–16); and it is seen most clearly in Jesus Christ (Rom. 3:21–22). As we see the righteousness of God clearly revealed in the cross of Christ, we can trust that his judgments on the wicked and oppressors will come eventually and will set creation to right (Rom. 8:20–21).

▶ Personal Implications

Take time to reflect on the implications of Ecclesiastes 3:16–4:16 for your own life today. Consider what you have learned that might lead you to praise God, repent of sin, and trust in his gracious promises. Make notes below on the personal implications for your walk with the Lord of the (1) *Gospel Glimpses*, (2) *Whole-Bible Connections*, (3) *Theological Soundings*, and (4) this passage as a whole.

1. Gospel Glimpses

2. Whole-Bible Connections

3. Theological Soundings

4. Ecclesiastes 3:16–4:16

> ## As You Finish This Unit . . .

Take a moment now to ask for the Lord's blessing and help as you continue in this study of Ecclesiastes. And take a moment also to look back through this unit of study, to reflect on some things that the Lord may be teaching you—and perhaps to highlight and underline these things to review again in the future

Definitions

[1] **Law** – When spelled with an initial capital letter, "Law" refers to the first five books of the Bible (Pentateuch). The Law contains numerous commands of God to his people, including the Ten Commandments and instructions regarding worship, sacrifice, and daily life in Israel. The NT often uses "the law" (lower case) to refer to the entire body of precepts set forth in the books of the Law.

[2] **Mediator** – One who intercedes between parties to resolve a conflict or achieve a goal. Jesus is the mediator between God and rebellious humanity (1 Tim. 2:5; compare Heb. 9:15; 12:24).

WEEK 6: FEAR GOD

Ecclesiastes 5:1–7

▲

The Place of the Passage

While it is wise to seek God, the Preacher reminds his readers that God is transcendent and is to be feared. Coming before God is no trivial matter, for, as the Preacher writes, "God is in heaven and you are on earth" (5:2)—a way of reminding readers that they are "under the sun," where everything is vanity. Therefore, those who would come before God should be circumspect, choosing their words carefully. Words that are spoken must be honored. There is no room for vanity before God.

The Big Picture

Because of God's holy and righteous character, we should fear him. There is no room for vanity in his presence.

> ## Reflection and Discussion

Read the entire text for this week's study, Ecclesiastes 5:1–7. Then review the following questions and write your notes on them concerning this section of Ecclesiastes. (For further background, see the *ESV Study Bible*, page 1202, or visit esv.org.)

1. In 3:9–15, the Preacher reflected on why people fear God as sovereign king of the universe. In 5:1–7, he again turns his attention to fearing God. What motivates the encouragement to "fear God"?

2. In the time of Ecclesiastes, a vow was an oath[1] sworn by a worshiper to perform a specific act in return for a favorable response from God. What examples in the Old Testament do you find of individuals making vows? Why might the Preacher make the recommendations of 5:4–6 to those making vows?

3. Why is it important to be careful with our "many words" (5:3)? Where else in the Bible do we find such warnings?

Read through the following three sections on *Gospel Glimpses*, *Whole-Bible Connections*, and *Theological Soundings*. Then take time to consider the *Personal Implications* these sections may have for you.

Gospel Glimpses

PROMISES MADE, PROMISES KEPT. The Preacher wishes to keep people from uttering rash or meaningless words during their worship of God (vv. 1–2), particularly the careless taking of a religious vow as an act of piety (see Deut. 23:21–23). By taking a vow, a worshiper would promise to perform a specific act (such as making a sacrifice) if God would respond favorably to a particular petition (Gen. 28:20–22; Judg. 11:30–31; 1 Sam. 1:11). Since making a sacrifice was costly, however, people often looked for some excuse to avoid following through on their vow (e.g., Eccles. 5:6). In this passage we see the importance of keeping vows. When we make promises, we must be intent on keeping them. However, because we are fallen creatures who cannot control the future, we often fail to keep our vows. In contrast, the God we worship does control the future and is faithful to his promises. We see this supremely in the sending of his Son, Jesus. All of God's promises are fulfilled in Christ (2 Cor. 1:20); what God has promised, he will be faithful to fulfill to those who are in Christ by faith.

THE IMPORTANCE OF OBEDIENCE. After Israel was rescued from captivity in Egypt, God gave them the Ten Commandments to guide their behavior as his covenant people. Having a clear standard for behavior communicated the importance of obedience to God. However, it is clear from the history of Israel that obedience was not a consistent reality in the people's lives. By the end of the Historical Books, Israel has been exiled from the Promised Land due to their continued idolatry and disobedience. But God is faithful to his promises to their father Abraham, and through the prophets he promises a new day when people will be renewed in the covenant and will be capable of living in obedience (Jer. 33:14–26; Ezek. 37:1–6).

Whole-Bible Connections

OBEDIENCE BEFORE SACRIFICE. The idea of obedience before sacrifice is common in the Bible (e.g., Hos. 6:6; Matt. 9:13). We see its importance stretching all the way back to Cain and Abel (Genesis 4). While both offered sacrifices before God, it appears that only Abel was obedient in the manner in which he offered his sacrifice. Likewise, once Israel left Egypt and built the tabernacle, the punishment of Nadab and Abihu showed the importance of obedience; the Israelites were not to offer sacrifices just however they pleased (Leviticus 10). In the time of the judges and kings, although the sacrificial system was in place, the people's hearts were drifting away from God as their kings, starting with Solomon, led them into idolatry. Eventually, when we come to the prophets, God expresses his desire that he would rather have obedience than empty sacrifices (Hos. 6:6). Jesus reiterates this sentiment in the Gospels (Matt. 9:13), and because of his perfect sacrifice, the tabernacle and temple rituals are no longer necessary. As we relate to God, we see his desire for hearts that follow and obey, rather than merely participating in outward religious rituals.

THE POWER OF THE TONGUE. Beginning with the tower of Babel (Genesis 11), we see the power of the tongue in Scripture. When everyone spoke the same language, they were able to coordinate their efforts to build a tower to the heavens and make a name for themselves. The confusion of languages led to the scattering of the people. Throughout the rest of the Old Testament, we see the power of the tongue for good or evil. It is a major theme in Proverbs, in reference to both the appropriate use of words (10:14; 11:12, 13; 12:18; 13:3, 16; 15:28; 17:27, 28; 19:1; 20:18, 25; 26:4) and the importance of speaking and listening (6:16–19; 8:6–9, 12–14; and numerous references in chapters 10–31). The Preacher in Ecclesiastes is working within this wisdom tradition in warning readers not to make hasty pronouncements (Eccles. 5:2, 6). Elsewhere, in the Prophets we are warned about the dangers of the tongue (Isa. 57:4, 59:3; Jer. 9:8; 18:18; Mic. 6:12). In the New Testament, James picks up this wisdom tradition and warns of the need to control the tongue (James 1:26) because of its power to destroy or to send mixed messages (3:1–12). Ultimately, all tongues will be brought under the lordship of Christ (Phil. 2:10–11) and will be used only for speaking good, not evil.

Theological Soundings

TEMPLE OF GOD AND PRESENCE OF GOD. In his speech in Acts, Stephen turns to the golden era of Israel, the days of David and Solomon, to make the point that the Jews have mistakenly associated God's presence solely with the temple.[2] By God's own words, he is not limited to a structure made with human hands (Acts 7:49–50). God is near to all who call on him (Ps. 145:18) and has drawn near to us most fully in Jesus Christ, the Righteous One. In the Old Testament, God made his dwelling among the Jews in the form of the tabernacle, a temporary tent that allowed Israel to say, "The glory of God is with us" (see Ex. 40:34–35). In the incarnation of Christ, God came to dwell among us, taking on flesh so that we may truly call him Immanuel, God with us (Matt. 1:23; John 1:14). As such, Jesus passed judgment on the temple as the focal point of covenant worship (Matt. 21:13; 23:38; 24:2) and pointed to himself as its replacement (Matt. 12:6; 26:61; 27:40, 51). He is that toward which the temple buildings always pointed. In him we meet with God, a communion that the temple was created to facilitate. Through Jesus' death, we have a perfect and permanent sacrifice[3] and intercessor for our sins (Heb. 7:23–28), as well as the gift of the Spirit who dwells within all who worship God in Spirit and in truth (John 4:23–24; Eph. 2:13–22).

CHRIST'S OBEDIENCE. Theologians often make a distinction between the active and passive obedience of Jesus. Active obedience focuses on the perfect life Christ lived while on earth. In line with the above emphasis on the importance of obedience, Jesus perfectly followed the commands of God. Passive obedience refers to his submission to sacrificial suffering and death on the cross. In this he followed the specific call of God on his life that brought together obedience and sacrifice. While the Old Testament emphasis was on obedience over sacrifice, in the New Testament God gave us, in Christ, a perfect sacrifice who also exhibited perfect obedience.

Personal Implications

Take time to reflect on the implications of Ecclesiastes 5:1–7 for your own life today. Consider what you have learned that might lead you to praise God, repent of sin, and trust in his gracious promises. Make notes below on the personal implications for your walk with the Lord of the (1) *Gospel Glimpses*, (2) *Whole-Bible Connections*, (3) *Theological Soundings*, and (4) this passage as a whole.

1. Gospel Glimpses

2. Whole-Bible Connections

3. Theological Soundings

----

4. Ecclesiastes 5:1–7

▶ As You Finish This Unit . . .

Take a moment now to ask for the Lord's blessing and help as you continue in this study of Ecclesiastes. And take a moment also to look back through this unit of study, to reflect on some things that the Lord may be teaching you—and perhaps to highlight and underline these things to review again in the future

Definitions

[1] **Oath** – Humans were warned in the OT not to swear promises rashly or falsely (Lev. 5:4; 19:11–12). Sometimes oaths were made in God's name, as though to guarantee them, but Jesus told his disciples not to swear oaths at all. Rather, they should let their simple statement of "yes" mean yes and their "no" mean no (Matt. 5:33–37).

[2] **Temple** – A place set aside as holy because of God's presence there. Solomon built the first temple of the Lord in Jerusalem, to replace the portable tabernacle. This temple was later destroyed by the Babylonians, rebuilt after the exile, and destroyed again by the Romans.

[3] **Sacrifice** – An offering to God, often to signify forgiveness of sin. The law of Moses gave detailed instructions regarding various kinds of sacrifices. By his death on the cross, Jesus gave himself as a sacrifice to atone for the sins of believers (Eph. 5:2; Heb. 10:12). Believers are to offer their bodies as living sacrifices to God (Rom. 12:1).

Week 7: Greed and Contentment

Ecclesiastes 5:8–6:9

The Place of the Passage

We should not be surprised, the Preacher says, to see injustice and oppression in this life. Those without power are at the mercy of those above them, for everyone is concerned with his own gain. Yet this is not enough for a good life. A greedy person will often lose everything in his pursuit of even more wealth, leaving his family destitute. Instead, the Preacher says, we must learn to enjoy what God has provided, rejoicing in life. It would be better to be dead than to be perpetually dissatisfied. In the end, all people will die. Therefore, it would be far better to learn contentment in this life than to be ruled by greed.

The Big Picture

Those who pursue wealth are never satisfied; it is far better to learn to be content with what you have and enjoy life.

> ### Reflection and Discussion

Read through the complete passage for this study, Ecclesiastes 5:8–6:9. Then review the questions below and record your notes and reflections on this section of Ecclesiastes. (For further background, see the *ESV Study Bible*, pages 1202–1203, or visit esv.org.)

1. In 5:10–6:9, the Preacher observes the destructive nature of greed. What does the Preacher conclude?

How does this compare with Paul's teachings, specifically in 1 Timothy 6 and Philippians 4?

2. How can we avoid being never-satisfied lovers of money (5:10) yet still enjoy the gifts of God discussed in verses 18–20? What does it mean to "not much remember" the days of one's life as God keeps us occupied with joy in our hearts (v. 20)?

3. In the time of Ecclesiastes, living a long life and having many children were among the highest of all earthly blessings. Where else in the Old Testament do you find long life and many children described as blessings? What does the Preacher conclude about these blessings in 6:3–6?

4. Who does the Preacher say has it worse in life than a stillborn child? Why is this?

Read through the following three sections on *Gospel Glimpses*, *Whole-Bible Connections*, and *Theological Soundings*. Then take time to consider the *Personal Implications* these sections may have for you.

Gospel Glimpses

GRACE AND GENEROSITY. In this passage we see that the days of our lives and the possessions we have are gifts from God (5:18–19). These gifts are a sign of God's common grace, something he provides for all his creatures. As believers, God's grace both saves and provides for us, allows for contentment, and gives a future. It also leads to our giving of grace to others in generosity and excludes the need to hoard and withhold forgiveness. As we recognize God's good and gracious gifts to us, we are able to take joy in them in giving to others.

OLD AGE AND THE AGE TO COME. In the Old Testament era, long life and numerous children were considered some of the highest of all earthly blessings (e.g., Gen. 15:15; Psalm 127). Yet even as good gifts from God, the days of our lives and of our children are still just a vapor. This leaves a longing within us

49

WEEK 7: GREED AND CONTENTMENT

for a permanence we cannot achieve in the here and now. Our longings point us to the promise of eternal life offered by God through Christ (1 John 5:11–12). The life we now enjoy and the fellowship we share with our families are foreshadowings of the joy that will be found when we live forever in the new heavens and the new earth (Revelation 21–22).

> ## Whole-Bible Connections

INJUSTICE UNDER THE SUN. The effects of the fall extend to human relationships (see Genesis 4), and thus in a fallen world one suffers outright injustice and wickedness at the hand of other human beings. One need only read the Old Testament, especially Judges, to see humans repeatedly "doing what is right in their own eyes" (see Judg. 21:25) to the detriment of other humans. In Psalms, the cries of God's people assure us that what makes this sad reality tolerable is the certainty that God will judge both the righteous and the wicked—that ultimately, justice will be done (Ps. 10:17–18). Reading from the end, we find this hope confirmed as John paints the picture of God executing final judgment (Rev. 20:11–21:8). In the meantime, though, we live in a world where we must endure much injustice (John 16:33), and the Preacher in Ecclesiastes speaks to this reality.

GREED AND CONTENTMENT. The Preacher observes the destructive nature of greed and concludes that contentment is a key characteristic of the godly life in this world (see Phil. 4:11; 1 Tim. 6:6, 8; Heb. 13:5). Back in the garden, Adam and Eve had everything they needed but were cast out because they chose to eat from the one tree that was off-limits. From that point on, the desire for more haunted the Old Testament. Especially in the life of Israel, the test set before them was whether they would be content with the good gifts and boundaries given by God or would seek fulfillment elsewhere. In the New Testament, Jesus warned about the deceitfulness of riches (Matt. 6:24; 13:22; Luke 12:15) and the futility of greed (Matt. 19:22–24; Luke 12:16–20). Moreover, he admonished us to be "rich toward God" (Luke 12:21), to seek first his kingdom (Luke 12:31), and to trust and thank God for provision (Matt. 6:19–33). Following Jesus (1 Tim. 6:3), Paul speaks of the damnable dangers of the love of money (v. 10) and the uncertainty of riches, and he charges wealthy Christians to "set their hopes . . . on God, who richly provides us with everything to enjoy" (v. 17).

JOY AND REJOICING. Common throughout Scripture is the theme of joy and rejoicing. Though not mentioned directly in Genesis 1–11, joy is an implied response on the part of humans to the good world God originally gave them. In the feasts established for Israel in the Pentateuch, we see the continued need to rejoice and show thanks for God's provisions (e.g., Deut. 12:7). Here in Ecclesiastes 5:18–20, we see the theme continued, and Jeremiah picks it up later by proclaiming a future time of rejoicing for those who are mourning (Jer. 31:13). In the New Testament, Mary rejoices in God before Jesus is born (Luke 1:46–55), and in one of Jesus' parables that most clearly depicts the gospel, a father rejoices over his prodigal son returning home (Luke 15:11–32). Revelation 19:7 completes the biblical picture, looking forward to the marriage supper of the Lamb.

Theological Soundings

PROVIDENCE OF GOD. God's providence is his continuing and often unseen activity in sustaining the universe. In a general sense, God sustains the created order, as he promised Noah after the flood (Gen. 8:22). In doing this, he holds all things together and controls the elements (Neh. 9:6; Job 37:1–17; Ps. 147:8; Isa. 40:26; Matt. 5:45; Acts 17:25–28; Col. 1:17; Heb. 1:3). Because of his providence in sustaining the created order, all life is ultimately dependent on God (Job 1:21; Ps. 127:3; Eccles. 3:2; 9:9; Ezek. 24:16; Dan. 5:26; Matt. 4:4; 10:29; 1 Tim. 6:13). In a particular sense, God focuses his providence on providing for his creatures (Job 38:39–41; Ps. 145:15–16; Luke 12:6–7; Acts 14:17; 1 Tim. 6:17). Because God provides for us, our response is to trust and find our contentment in him.

COMMON GRACE. Many Christians tend to think of grace only in terms of God's movements toward us for our salvation. Indeed, we see God's grace supremely in the cross of Christ and the giving of his Holy Spirit to believers. However, this is not all there is to grace. Much like God's general and special revelation, we can speak of God's general (or common) and special grace. God's common grace is available to all as he gives humankind blessings in addition to those related to salvation. From a Christian perspective, physical provision (Matt. 5:44–45; Acts 14:16–17), science and technological innovations, legal systems (Rom. 2:14–15), the arts (Ex. 31:1–16), and even the growth and development of human society (Gen. 5:4; 9:6; Rom. 13:1–4) in general are all signs of God's common grace. Common grace is ultimately a demonstration of the goodness and mercy of God that brings him glory as he governs and provides for his human creatures.

Personal Implications

Take time to reflect on the implications of Ecclesiastes 5:8–6:9 for your own life today. Consider what you have learned that might lead you to praise God, repent of sin, and trust in his gracious promises. Make notes below on the personal implications for your walk with the Lord of the (1) *Gospel Glimpses*, (2) *Whole-Bible Connections*, (3) *Theological Soundings*, and (4) this passage as a whole.

1. Gospel Glimpses

2. Whole-Bible Connections

3. Theological Soundings

4. Ecclesiastes 5:8–6:9

As You Finish This Unit . . .

Take a moment now to ask for the Lord's blessing and help as you continue in this study of Ecclesiastes. And take a moment also to look back through this unit of study, to reflect on some things that the Lord may be teaching you—and perhaps to highlight and underline these things to review again in the future.

Week 8: The Contrast of Wisdom and Folly

Ecclesiastes 6:10–7:29

The Place of the Passage

The opening verses of chapter 7 contain beautiful and evocative descriptions of both wisdom and folly. The Preacher describes the benefits of wise living as priceless, while a life of foolishness is easy to come by. The Preacher says that he has seen everything life has to offer. He has seen both good and wicked people, and the power that lies within wisdom. Yet the Preacher acknowledges that he is rarely able to truly understand the people he encounters. He concludes that while "God made man upright" (7:29), everyone is consumed with their own desires and schemes.

The Big Picture

In the face of "vanity," it is still possible to know and do what is good.

> ## Reflection and Discussion

Read through the complete passage for this study, Ecclesiastes 6:10–7:29. Then review the questions below concerning this section of Ecclesiastes and write your notes on them. (For further background, see the *ESV Study Bible*, pages 1203–1204, or visit esv.org.)

1. Wisdom for Living "Under the Sun" (6:10–7:24)

In Genesis 2:19–20, Adam is granted the ability to name every living creature, "and whatever the man called every living creature, that was its name." In naming, a connection is formed between name and identity—to be named is to be known. Look at Psalm 91:14–15, where the psalmist reveals what trusting in God looks like. How does this compare with how the Preacher in Ecclesiastes views naming and God's sovereignty (6:10–11)?

In Ecclesiastes 7:1 the Preacher says, "A good name is better than precious ointment, and the day of death than the day of birth." What does the day of death refer to? Why is mourning better than feasting, or sorrow better than laughter (vv. 2–3)?

In 7:11–12 the Preacher compares wisdom and money. In what ways are the two similar? How would a fool act? What would you say is the Preacher's general rule about wisdom?

Within the Old Testament, being righteous refers not only to ethical or moral behavior, but also to being "right" or "just" in one's cause. What examples can you find of this in the Old Testament, especially in the Pentateuch? What does the Preacher mean by exhorting us to "be not overly righteous" (7:16), and to "be not overly wicked" (v. 17)?

2. The Heart of the Problem: Sin (7:25–29)

In 7:25–29, the Preacher is unable to "find" (i.e., figure out or understand) human beings. What is his conclusion about humans? What does the Preacher offer as the cause or heart of the problem? To what important doctrine do verses 20, 25–29 point?

In light of Romans 8:20–23, where Paul describes the cursing of creation due to the fall, what is the tragic reality of the fall that the Preacher describes in Ecclesiastes 7:25–29?

_____

_____

_____

_____

Read through the following three sections on *Gospel Glimpses, Whole-Bible Connections,* and *Theological Soundings.* Then take time to consider the *Personal Implications* these sections may have for you.

Gospel Glimpses

JESUS IS THE EXCEPTION TO SIN. Mankind is scheming (Eccles. 7:27–29) and needs a Savior: Ecclesiastes affirms the Bible's view of sin (e.g., Rom. 3:9–10; Mark 7:20–23). We celebrate Jesus as the exception—"who in every respect has been tempted as we are, yet without sin" (Heb. 4:15)—and we rejoice that "for our sake [God] made him to be sin who knew no sin, so that in him we might become the righteousness of God" (2 Cor. 5:21). Also, the life of wisdom highlighted in the passage comes from the grace of the gospel: "The grace of God has appeared, bringing salvation for all people, training us to renounce ungodliness and worldly passions, and to live self-controlled, upright, and godly lives in the present age" (Titus 2:11–12).

COMFORT FOR THOSE WHO MOURN. The Preacher in Ecclesiastes talks about the value of mourning (7:2–4). While mourning is a feature of this life under the sun, there will eventually be no more mourning. In the Beatitudes, Jesus promised that those who mourn would be comforted (Matt. 5:4), and in the previous verse he promised that those who are poor in spirit would see the kingdom of heaven (v. 3). We see his compassion for those experiencing the negative effects of life under the sun, and he enters into that suffering to redeem us from it.

Whole-Bible Connections

PERVASIVENESS OF SIN. In some ways, the story of the Bible from Genesis 3 to Revelation 20 is the story of human sin. Only Daniel in the Old Testament appears for any length of time without showing some major flaw or shortcoming. The remaining characters all sin, sometimes habitually, easily proving Paul's sweeping assertion that all have sinned (Romans 3). The Preacher in Ecclesiastes is acutely aware of the pervasiveness of human sin. He sees the solution as following the path of wisdom, and this perspective is ultimately vindicated in the New Testament. Believers are called to follow Christ, in whom all the treasures of wisdom and knowledge are found (Col. 2:3). The pervasiveness of sin is finally dealt with only on the cross, as Christ became sin for us so that we might become "the righteousness of God" (2 Cor. 5:21).

THE VALUE OF WISDOM. The proverbs in Ecclesiastes 7 are clustered around the thematic words "good" or "better" (7:1, 2, 3, 5, 8, 10, 11, 18, 20), and they attempt to provide at least a partial answer to the question, "Who knows what is good for man?" From one perspective, even the greatest wisdom teachers cannot give infallible advice based upon an absolutely certain knowledge of what will be; nevertheless, the sanctified counsel of the wise is a useful source of guidance for ordinary living. Because of the futility that entered the world through the fall (Gen. 3:16–19), the counterintuitive is the wisest approach—trusting God over circumstances and appearances. That was God's original intention for humanity (Gen. 1:26–28). Such wisdom provides more protection than money and preserves life (and sanity) when this broken world makes no sense. Such brokenness can make our final days of pain seem more desirable than the day of our birth into this troubled existence. But this wisdom concludes ultimately that it is not within our knowledge or experience to make sense of what God does on an earthly plane. The Old Testament characters in the hall of faith (Hebrews 11) all did this to some extent, and Jesus is the supreme example of proving that the wisdom of God's ways is counterintuitive to the world (1 Cor. 1:18–31).

Theological Soundings

HUMAN SIN. The Preacher tells his readers, "Surely there is not a righteous man on earth who does good and never sins." This describes the depravity[1] of the human condition after the fall. Sin is anything (whether thought, action, or attitude) that does not express or conform to the holy character of God as expressed in his moral law. It is any violation of or failure to adhere to the commands of God, or the desire to do so. According to the Bible, "All have sinned and fall short of the glory of God" (Rom. 3:23), and "The wages of sin is death" (6:23). Only the death and resurrection of Jesus Christ has opened up the way for forgiveness of sins.

THEODICY. Christians affirm that there is one God (Deut. 6:4), who created the heavens and the earth (Genesis 1). We also affirm that he is all-powerful (Ps. 93:1), personal in his relationship to his creatures (e.g., his interactions with his people throughout Scripture), and ultimately and totally good (1 Tim. 4:4).

The current existence of sin and evil appears to make one or more of these beliefs problematic. The attempt to work through this apparent problem is called "theodicy," the defense of God in the face of sin and evil. The book of Job is more focused on this than Ecclesiastes, but here it is still a major topic. The solution in both cases is found in trusting in the character and wisdom of God. If God is all-wise in addition to the attributes listed above, he must have a good reason for allowing the sin and evil that does exist. Further, the cross of Christ shows that God is willing to go to great lengths to remedy the problem, so we can trust that he both cares for his children and knows what he is doing.

Personal Implications

Take time to reflect on the implications of Ecclesiastes 6:10–7:29 for your own life today. Consider what you have learned that might lead you to praise God, repent of sin, and trust in his gracious promises. Make notes below on the personal implications for your walk with the Lord of the (1) *Gospel Glimpses*, (2) *Whole-Bible Connections*, (3) *Theological Soundings*, and (4) this passage as a whole.

1. Gospel Glimpses

2. Whole-Bible Connections

3. Theological Soundings

4. Ecclesiastes 6:10–7:29

As You Finish This Unit . . .

Take a moment now to ask for the Lord's blessing and help as you continue in this study of Ecclesiastes. And take a moment also to look back through this unit of study, to reflect on some things that the Lord may be teaching you—and perhaps to highlight and underline these things to review again in the future.

Definition

[1] **Depravity** – The sinful condition of human nature apart from grace, whereby humans are inclined to serve their own will and desires and to reject God's rightful rule over them.

WEEK 9: IN THE HAND OF GOD

Ecclesiastes 8:1–9:12

The Place of the Passage

There is a tendency to assume that those in authority possess wisdom, but the Preacher reminds us that kings are like any other persons, except that they have the power to do great harm. This is why the Preacher is concerned that those who would counsel the king do so with wisdom. He has also observed that many people are inclined toward evil because God is slow to punish and therefore they assume there will be no punishment at all. But even though a sinner may extend his life through evil, only those who fear God can hope in him. For all must eventually "go to the dead" (9:3), no matter what they have done in life. The Preacher's advice is to work hard and enjoy life whenever possible. Do not trust in talents or wealth, intelligence or strength, because, writes the Preacher, everyone is subject to "time and chance" (9:11).

The Big Picture

All mankind is subject to the same fate of decay and death, but those who fear God have their hope in him.

> ## Reflection and Discussion

Read through the complete passage for this study, Ecclesiastes 8:1–9:12. Then review the questions below concerning this section of Ecclesiastes and write your notes on them. (For further background, see the *ESV Study Bible*, pages 1205–1206, or visit esv.org.)

1. Wisdom, Fearing God, and the Limits of Human Knowledge (8:1–17)

The Preacher presents two rhetorical questions at the beginning of chapter 8: "Who is like the wise? And who knows the interpretation of a thing?" What is the point of these rhetorical questions? How does this compare with Proverbs 2:1–4?

In Ecclesiastes 8:10–13, the Preacher returns to the concept of those who fear God. In 3:16; 4:1; and 5:8, he has already pointed out that people do not always get what they deserve in this life. What is the Preacher's solution to the reality that sometimes evil seems to prevail and bad things happen to the righteous? How does he arrive at this solution? What should our response be to these things?

In 8:14–15, the Preacher says it is "vanity" that the wicked appear to escape judgment[1] and instead receive blessings (8:10–13), and that there is no satisfying explanation for why the righteous receive the treatment due to the wicked. Since this mystery cannot be completely solved, one should not become so obsessed with attempting to unravel it that one neglects to enjoy Gods gifts (8:15). Compare 8:15 to 2:24; 3:12; 3:22; 5:17; 9:7–9a; and 11:7–12:1a. How might the Preacher's recommendation to pursue enjoyment relate to all that seems to be vanity?

----

2. Death Comes to All (9:1–12)

In what way does the phrase "in the hand of God" (9:1) offer security in the face of the reality that death comes to all? How does this relate to Deuteronomy 33:3?

Explain the phrase "a living dog is better than a dead lion" (Eccles. 9:4).

In 9:7–9, how does the Preacher advise us to live in light of the fact that death is a reality (vv. 1–6)?

63

Read through the following three sections on *Gospel Glimpses*, *Whole-Bible Connections*, and *Theological Soundings*. Then take time to consider the *Personal Implications* these sections may have for you.

Gospel Glimpses

FEASTING WITH GOD. The recommendation to enjoy eating and drinking as a gift from God (2:24; 3:13; 5:18; 8:15; 9:7) echoes the deeper invitation of eating and feasting with God. History begins and ends with a joyful feast in the presence of God. In Eden, God gave humanity "every tree that is pleasant to the sight and good for food" (Gen. 2:9, 16–17). Because Adam and Eve rejected this generosity, we are separated from God to eat in frustration (Gen. 3:19). Yet God is reopening the way to his festive table. He welcomed Israel's elders to Mount Sinai, where "they beheld God, and ate and drank" (Ex. 24:11). Through Isaiah he tells us that people from all nations will come to his table: God will "make for all peoples a feast of rich food, a feast of well-aged wine" (Isa. 25:6). Picking up on this promise, Jesus compared his coming kingdom to a wedding feast (Matt. 22:2; Luke 14:15–24) and provided signposts to it with his abundant provisions of food and wine (Mark 6:30–44; 8:1–10; John 2:1–11). As the redeemed eat the Lord's Supper, we enjoy an "appetizer" to the coming banquet, purchased by his death (Luke 22:14, 16). When Jesus returns, he will restore and "ratchet up" the feast of Eden, spreading a banquet for all who trust in him. "Blessed are those who are invited to the marriage supper of the Lamb" (Rev. 19:9).

LABOR NOT IN VAIN. Death is inevitable (2:16–17), coming to all (9:1–7). The despair in Ecclesiastes is due to God's curse on creation, most notably the reality of death. We are reminded that "the wages of sin is death" (Rom. 6:23; see Gen. 2:17). Through Christ's death and resurrection, we also know that death has lost its "sting," that we have "victory through our Lord Jesus Christ," that our "labor is not in vain" (1 Cor. 15:55–58), and that someday Jesus, as Creator of all, will reconcile us to God (Col. 1:15–20), reversing completely the curses of the fall (Rom. 8:19–22). Thus we affirm with Paul that "to die is gain" (Phil. 1:21; see 2 Cor. 5:2), because, as Jesus said, "whoever believes in [him], though he die, yet shall he live" (John 11:25; see Rom. 6:23b).

Whole-Bible Connections

RESPECT FOR GOD'S RULERS. In Ecclesiastes 8:2, the Preacher writes, "Keep the king's command, because of God's oath to him." Compare this with David, who also respected a divine office—that of king—even when held by a bad man, Saul. David intentionally avoided harming the Lord's anointed, even as Saul repeatedly attempted to kill him (1 Sam. 24:6). Obedience to God is seen in respect for his leaders, while resistance to God often is manifest in resentment of them. Joseph's brothers despised him when he told them of God's plan to exalt him (Gen. 37:5–8). The Psalms equate rebellion against God's anointed with rebellion against God (Ps. 2:2). Jesus, as God's true Anointed One, was despised and executed because the people rejected his office (Luke 19:14; 20:14–18).

FEASTING. In the face of vanity, the Preacher commends eating and drinking as a repeated refrain throughout Ecclesiastes (Eccles. 2:24; 3:13; 5:18; 8:15; 9:7). This involves the enjoyment of food and drink as the provision of God in an otherwise undependable world that is beyond human control, understanding, or anticipation. This theme started in the garden of Eden, where God provided food for Adam and Eve and invited them to eat. Israel was fed miraculously with manna in the wilderness. Such gracious provision comes to its richest fulfillment in the ministry of Jesus, who alone has mastery over the earthly elements. One thinks of his miracle at Cana (John 2:1–11), his dining at Matthew's house (Matt. 9:10–15), the feeding of the multitudes (Matt. 14:14–21; 15:32–38), the Last Supper (Mark 14:17–25), and the post-resurrection breakfast on the beach (John 21:12). Finally, we reflect on the future wedding supper of the Lamb (Rev. 19:9), which we anticipate each time we celebrate the Lord's Supper, proclaiming "the Lord's death *until he comes*" (1 Cor. 11:26).

DEATH DEFEATED. Death, like sin and sickness and sorrow, does not belong in this world that God created and declared "good" (Gen. 1:4, 10, etc.). Death is a curse, introduced in response to our rebellion against God (2:17). Yet we read in Isaiah that someday God "will swallow up death forever" (Isa. 25:8). When? This triumph began when Jesus walked out of his own tomb two thousand years ago. He "abolished death and brought life and immortality to light through the gospel" (2 Tim. 1:10). But we still await the complete victory. He will return, raise his people from their graves, and overthrow death, which will then become the "last enemy to be destroyed" (1 Cor. 15:26). Paul celebrates this with an allusion to Isaiah's promise: "Then shall come to pass the saying that is written: 'Death is swallowed up in victory'" (1 Cor. 15:54; see Isa. 25:8).

Theological Soundings

COMMUNION. Among Christian denominations, the practice of communion, or the Lord's Supper, is variously understood, but all denominations agree that it is a key focal point of Christian worship. The institution of a meal commemorating redemption goes back to the Passover in Exodus (Exodus 12). Later, in the New Testament Jesus celebrates Passover with his disciples on the night he is betrayed (Luke 22:7–13) and establishes that the meal should now be done in remembrance of his impending sacrifice (vv. 8–20). We infer from Paul's letter to the Corinthians that celebrating the Lord's Supper was standard early church practice (1 Cor. 11:17–34). While the exact nature of the practice varies from church to church now, it is still a vital reminder and a means of grace whereby we remember Christ's work for us and look forward to sharing the "marriage supper of the Lamb" with him at his second coming (Rev. 19:9).

RESURRECTION. Resurrection is not a major Old Testament theme, but there are hints and shadows nevertheless. Abraham's willingness to sacrifice Isaac seems to involve hope in the boy's returning to life (Gen. 22:5; Heb. 11:19). Elsewhere there is reference to hope of resurrection (Ps. 16:8–11; Dan. 12:2), as well as literal resurrections (e.g., 1 Kings 17:22; 2 Kings 4:35). With Christ's resurrection in the New Testament, everything changes. In John's Gospel, Christ's resurrection is the final sign vindicating him as the Son of God (John 20:30–31). Christ's death and resurrection were central to the gospel proclamation in the New Testament (Acts 2:24; 3:15; 10:40; 13:29–30) and are prominent in the teaching of Paul. Christ's resurrection is the basis of faith (1 Cor. 15:14–15; Rom. 10:9; 2 Tim. 2:8), justification (Rom. 4:25; 8:34), Christian hope (1 Cor. 15:19), and ultimately our own future resurrection (vv. 20–23). It is the ultimate answer to the fact that death is inevitable, and it reveals how sin and death are ultimately done away with and defeated for good.

> ## Personal Implications

Take time to reflect on the implications of Ecclesiastes 8:1–9:12 for your own life today. Consider what you have learned that might lead you to praise God, repent of sin, and trust in his gracious promises. Make notes below on the personal implications for your walk with the Lord of the (1) *Gospel Glimpses*, (2) *Whole-Bible Connections*, (3) *Theological Soundings*, and (4) this passage as a whole.

1. Gospel Glimpses

2. Whole-Bible Connections

3. Theological Soundings

4. Ecclesiastes 8:1–9:12

> ### As You Finish This Unit . . .

Take a moment now to ask for the Lord's blessing and help as you continue in this study of Ecclesiastes. And take a moment also to look back through this unit of study, to reflect on some things that the Lord may be teaching you—and perhaps to highlight and underline these things to review again in the future.

Definition

[1] **Judgment** – Any assessment of something or someone, especially moral assessment. The Bible also speaks of a final day of judgment when Christ returns, when all those who have refused to repent will be judged (Rev. 20:12–15).

WEEK 10: WISDOM IS BETTER THAN FOLLY

Ecclesiastes 9:13–12:7

▲

The Place of the Passage

Wisdom can achieve greatness and surpasses many priceless gifts, but just a little folly overwhelms whatever good has been achieved. In 10:8–11, the Preacher reminds us that folly is not always intentional; it is often the result of carelessness, which is second nature to the fool. The Preacher says the wise will act wisely and fools will choose folly. Yet no one is doomed to be a fool, and no one is guaranteed to be wise. The Preacher says it is good to enjoy one's youth. Indeed, he declares youth as the best time to remember God, when people are strong and fit, rather than when they are old, bent, and miserable.

The Big Picture

It is good to remember God when you are young and life is good, but do not forget that all life is vanity, leading inevitably to death and judgment.

> ### Reflection and Discussion

Read through the complete passage for this study, Ecclesiastes 9:13–12:7. Then review the questions below concerning this section of Ecclesiastes and write your notes on them. (For further background, see the *ESV Study Bible*, pages 1206–1209, or visit esv.org.)

1. The Paths of Wisdom and Foolishness (9:13–11:6)

In 9:13–18, the Preacher presents examples of wisdom's ability to produce great results. What happens if wisdom is forgotten or despised? How does the value of wisdom compare with might, and why? What does the Preacher say about wisdom in verses 13–18?

In 10:2 the Preacher says, "A wise man's heart inclines him to the right, but a fool's heart to the left." Read Exodus 15:6 and 15:12; Psalms 16:11 and 17:7; and Isaiah 41:10. In light of these verses, what do the references to "right" and "left" mean in Ecclesiastes 10:2?

How do verses 10:1–20 fit together? To what book of the Old Testament is this section similar?

What might it mean to "cast your bread upon the waters" (11:1)? What is the central point of 11:1–6? What wisdom is suggested in verses 2 and 6?

2. Aging and the Vanity of Mortal Life (11:7–12:7)

In 7:1–4 the Preacher said that being confronted with others' mortality causes one to grow in spiritual wisdom. In 11:7–12:7, the Preacher urges us to embrace wisdom in view of what?

What does the Preacher recommend in 11:9, given the fact that "God will bring you into judgment"? What is proper rejoicing or enjoyment of life?

In light of the inevitability of aging and "evil days" (12:1), how does the Preacher advise us to respond?

In 12:2–7 the Preacher presents a metaphorical description of the aging process and death. Which items seem to resemble specific aspects of aging? The common link between the objects in verse 6 is their use as receptacles for water. Looking at 2 Samuel 14:14; John 4:14; and Revelation 21:6; 22:1; 22:17, what is water a symbol for, and how does the destruction of the objects in Ecclesiastes 12:6 relate to the aging process?

Read through the following three sections on *Gospel Glimpses, Whole-Bible Connections*, and *Theological Soundings*. Then take time to consider the *Personal Implications* these sections may have for you.

Gospel Glimpses

BEING FAITHFUL WITHOUT KNOWING THE FUTURE. It is encouraging to know that it is "God who works in you, both to will and to work for his good pleasure" (Phil. 2:13). Ecclesiastes 11:1–6 highlights the fact that we do not need to know the future or understand everything in order to know that God's work will be done. We can work hard and be generous without knowing all the answers or understanding every detail of *why* we are working hard and being generous—it is enough to be faithful. Compare 2 Corinthians 9:6–11: "Whoever sows sparingly will also reap sparingly, and whoever sows bountifully will also reap bountifully. . . . God is able to make all grace abound to you, so that having all sufficiency in all things at all times, you may abound in every good work. . . . He who supplies seed to the sower and bread for food will supply and multiply your seed for sowing and increase the harvest of your righteousness. You will be enriched in every way to be generous in every way, which through us will produce thanksgiving to God."

SOLACE IN GOD. Youth and the dawn of life reflect God's good creation, but the fall (Genesis 3) has ensured that there will be many "days of darkness" (Eccles. 11:8). Because of this, we must remember our Creator and not idolize our days of glory. Ultimate wholeness is found in Christ, not in a broken creation. The imperative to "Remember also your Creator" (12:1) invites us to depend on our Creator for solace in a broken world. This reminder will ultimately move us forward in our search for wholeness to the culminating truths of salvation history revealed in Jesus (John 1:1–3; 20:17, 30–31), for it is in Christ that we see God's promise of abundant life (John 10:10) and the renewal of all things (Rev. 21:5).

Whole-Bible Connections

WHEN FOLLY RULES. This section is somewhat loosely organized, but two contrasting key themes throughout are "wisdom" (9:13, 15–18; 10:1–2, 10, 12) and "folly" (9:17; 10:1–3, 6, 12–15). The "wise" and the "fool" are two of the three main characters in the book of Proverbs. Elsewhere, the general movement of the monarchial period in Israel's history is from wisdom to folly. First Kings begins with the wisest man in the known world ruling Israel, before his gradual movement away from the "fear of the Lord" leads to increasing folly for him and his descendants. Israel's folly leads ultimately to the exile. While the Wisdom Literature outlines what is needed to pursue true wisdom, it is often folly that rules the day. The idea of folly "set in many high places" (10:6) is borne out in all the foolish rulers in the Bible, from the evil kings in the Old Testament to the Jewish leaders who crucified Jesus and persecuted the church in the New Testament. Humanity ultimately needs a wise ruler not prone to folly, a hope that will be realized in Christ's return to establish fully his rule and reign.

THE GROANING OF CREATION. Although creation was originally created good (see Theological Soundings, below), it has been groaning since the fall of man placed it under a curse (Gen. 3:16–19). This section in Ecclesiastes reflects this theme, which resonates elsewhere in the Wisdom Literature (Job 14:1–2; 23:2). Jeremiah picks up the theme in his prophecy when he asks how long the land will mourn and remain desolate (Jer. 12:4, 11). Paul discusses the solution to the problem in the redemption of not only humanity but the created order as a whole (Rom. 8:19–23). This is made possible through Christ's death and resurrection, which inaugurates the new creation (1 Cor. 15:20–28). Through Christ, not only our bodies are redeemed, but the creation itself. At his second coming, Christ will establish his kingdom fully on this earth and the presence of God will cover the earth as the waters cover the sea (Hab. 2:14), finally eradicating the groaning, and restoring creation to its original intended goodness.

Theological Soundings

CHRIST AS WISDOM. Wisdom is given high praise in this passage (9:13–18) and elsewhere in Scripture. This could be problematic unless wisdom is understood in close connection with God himself. Ultimately, all the treasures of wisdom and knowledge are found in Christ alone (Col. 2:3). If that is true, then the search for wisdom in the Old Testament books of Job, Ecclesiastes, Song of Solomon, Proverbs, and Psalms is really a search for Christ. This may be easier to recognize in passages like Proverbs 8:22–36, where wisdom is personified and connected with the creation of the world. Later, in the New Testament, Paul explains that by Christ all things were created and are now held together (Col. 1:16–17). Elsewhere, Paul makes explicit that Christ is the wisdom of God (1 Cor. 1:30).

THE GOODNESS OF CREATION. In order to have a fully Christian understanding of the surrounding world, we must look at it first as the creation of a Creator (Genesis 1–2). The world is not just a brute fact of existence. Likewise, it is not a cosmic accident, implying no ultimate purpose beyond what we make of it. Instead, we believe the world is God's direct creation and he continues to be involved in it. According to Genesis 1, the world as initially created by God was good. This does not necessarily mean "good" in a moral sense; rather, it is an affirmation that the creation is not inherently damaged. The damage and evil that do exist are the result of man's rebellion against his Creator (Genesis 3), but creation is not so devastated as to be beyond any good. Creation was originally good and is now marred, but one day it will be restored and advanced beyond God's original intentions for Eden (Revelation 21–22). In the meantime, creation is not an evil to overcome. This world is our home; we are not just passing through. But it is a home in need of renovation, and one day we will see that hope realized.

Personal Implications

Take time to reflect on the implications of Ecclesiastes 9:13–12:7 for your own life today. Consider what you have learned that might lead you to praise God, repent of sin, and trust in his gracious promises. Make notes below on the personal implications for your walk with the Lord of the (1) *Gospel Glimpses*, (2) *Whole-Bible Connections*, (3) *Theological Soundings*, and (4) this passage as a whole.

1. Gospel Glimpses

2. Whole-Bible Connections

3. Theological Soundings

4. Ecclesiastes 9:13–12:7

As You Finish This Unit . . .

Take a moment now to ask for the Lord's blessing and help as you continue in this study of Ecclesiastes. And take a moment also to look back through this unit of study, to reflect on some things that the Lord may be teaching you—and perhaps to highlight and underline these things to review again in the future.

Week 11: Remember Your Creator

Ecclesiastes 12:8–14

The Place of the Passage

The Preacher sought out wisdom, taught all that he knew, and painstakingly arranged this book. He made wisdom the goal of his life, and this is his conclusion after all his struggles: all that is expected of mankind is to fear God and keep his commandments.[1] God will bring every deed into judgment, including every secret thing. This opens up the possibility that there is more going on in life than what we can see—we should not assume we know all our own desires or secrets. No matter how wise we become, only God sees all.

The Big Picture

Fear God and keep his commandments.

Reflection and Discussion

Read through the complete passage for this study, Ecclesiastes 12:8–14. Then review the questions below concerning this section of Ecclesiastes and write your notes on them. (For further background, see the *ESV Study Bible*, page 1209, or visit esv.org.)

1. In 12:11, the Preacher references a "goad," a long stick normally used to guide oxen while plowing. What does the Preacher say about the "words of the wise" and their origin?

2. Read Psalm 80:1; Ezekiel 34:23; and John 10:11, 16. Who is the "one Shepherd" referred to here?

3. According to Ecclesiastes 12:13–14, what is the Preacher's ultimate conclusion, and how does it fit with what has been said previously? What is the inevitable result of true faith[2]?

Read through the following three sections on *Gospel Glimpses*, *Whole-Bible Connections*, and *Theological Soundings*. Then take time to consider the *Personal Implications* these sections may have for you.

Gospel Glimpses

ONE SHEPHERD. The passage shows that God is the one true shepherd of his people, who provides them with wisdom. This reality is fulfilled in Christ the Good Shepherd. If the writer is borrowing from the language of Ezekiel (Ezek. 34:23–24; 37:24–25), the reference to "one shepherd" serves as an anticipation of the coming Davidic shepherd king. The New Testament identifies this as Jesus (Matt. 25:31–46), who called himself "one shepherd" (John 10:16), as well as the "good shepherd" who laid "down [his] life for the sheep" (vv. 14–15).

ONE JUDGE. In addition to being our Shepherd, Jesus is also the future judge and our future hope. If you have yet to realize that God is the Ruler of this exceedingly complex universe—and that therefore *you* are not—the door to the kingdom of heaven[3] and a meaningful life remains closed. To you, this verse serves as a final warning, with the weight of the warning falling on the words "every" and "secret." Each and every word, action, and thought will be judged by God (see 12:14; Rom. 2:16). However, if you have come to Christ in faith and are thus willing to live in dependence upon his wisdom, provision, and grace, this verse serves as a reminder of the comfort that will come when Jesus balances the scales of justice on the last day. On that day he will vindicate those already declared righteous by him. He will also condemn the wicked, who, by rejecting him, will have every deed, including every secret thing, taken into account (Matt. 25:31–46; 2 Cor. 5:10).

Whole-Bible Connections

GOD AS SHEPHERD. The idea of God (and Jesus) as shepherd is common in Scripture. Probably the most well-known reference to this is Psalm 23. However, the majority of references to shepherds are in the Pentateuch and the Prophets. In the Pentateuch, it is mainly a literal reference to shepherding (e.g., Gen. 29:3; 26:19–22; 46:32; Ex. 22:5). In the Prophets, the reference takes on metaphorical connotations as a way of referring to the leaders of God's people (e.g., Jer. 23:1–5; 50:6). Shepherds are required to display a unique combination of strength and warmth as they tend to their sheep's needs while also protecting them from predators. This makes an illuminating way to understand the ways of God with his people. God is the ultimate shepherd, and Jesus explains how he has made that image incarnate (John 10:1–18). The author of Hebrews picks up this imagery (Heb. 13:20), as does the apostle Peter (1 Pet. 2:25; 5:4), in explaining how Jesus cares for us.

FEAR OF THE LORD. In Ecclesiastes we see that all is vanity. This should drive people to take refuge in God, whose work "endures forever" (3:14) and who is a "rock" for those who take shelter in him (e.g., Pss. 18:2; 62:8; 94:22). In other words, it summons people to "fear" or "revere" God. In some sense, "fearing" is a by-product of recognizing Christ as Lord. In the beginning of Proverbs, we are told that the beginning of wisdom is to fear the Lord (Prov. 1:1–7). This fear of the Lord implies that God is to be revered and respected, and the best way that we can show this respect for our Lord is by keeping his commandments (Deut. 6:1–3). Throughout Scripture, God's people are to fear and respect him, but that is not antithetical to love (Deut. 6:4–6). This emphasis is picked up in the New Testament by the apostle John (John 14:15; 1 John 2:3) and is encouraged by the author of Hebrews in his explanation of God as final judge (Heb. 4:12). Our fear of God culminates in obedience and worship, the earmarks of life in heaven (Rev. 5:9–14).

Theological Soundings

THE WISDOM OF GOD. Ecclesiastes 1:12–18 reflects the quest for wisdom in other Wisdom Literature (e.g., Ps. 90:12; Prov. 4:5). The one who toils only to give the fruit of his labor to others (Eccles. 2:18–23) is reminiscent of the parable of the rich fool in Luke 12:16–20. On the limits of wisdom, see also 1 Corinthians 1:18–31. On the bankruptcy of self-indulgence, see Galatians 5:16–17 and 1 John 2:15–17. Like the Preacher of Ecclesiastes, Jesus was a wisdom teacher, surpassing even Solomon in his wisdom (Matt. 12:42). Jesus also lived a life of wisdom. From the cradle to the cross he walked the way of wisdom. Denying himself the usual rewards of godliness—long life, good reputation, strong marriage, healthy children, material prosperity—he submitted to the wise but inexplicable will of his Father, enduring a humiliating death, so that in his sufferings he might become for us the very wisdom and power of God (1 Cor. 1:24).

CHRIST'S RETURN AND FINAL JUDGMENT. Someday Christ will return in great glory, and there will be a definitive, comprehensive acknowledgment that he is Lord over all. He will then judge the living and the dead. All people and forces that oppose him will be vanquished, including death itself (Matt. 25:31; 1 Cor. 15:24–28), "so that at the name of Jesus every knee should bow, in heaven and on earth and under the earth, and every tongue confess that Jesus Christ is Lord, to the glory of God the Father" (Phil. 2:10–11).

Personal Implications

Take time to reflect on the implications of Ecclesiastes 12:8–14 for your own life today. Consider what you have learned that might lead you to praise God, repent of sin, and trust in his gracious promises. Make notes below on the personal implications for your walk with the Lord of the (1) *Gospel Glimpses*, (2) *Whole-Bible Connections*, (3) *Theological Soundings*, and (4) this passage as a whole.

1. Gospel Glimpses

2. Whole-Bible Connections

3. Theological Soundings

4. Ecclesiastes 12:8–14

As You Finish This Unit . . .

Take a moment now to ask for the Lord's blessing and help as you continue in this study of Ecclesiastes. And take a moment also to look back through this unit of study, to reflect on some things that the Lord may be teaching you—and perhaps to highlight and underline these things to review again in the future.

Definitions

[1] **Commandment** – In the Bible, an instruction or order given by God. Commandments appear throughout Scripture, but most occur in the Law, the first five books of the Bible. Most famous are the Ten Commandments (Ex. 20:2–17; Deut. 5:6–21).

[2] **Faith** – Trust in or reliance upon something or someone despite a lack of concrete proof. Salvation, which is purely a work of God's grace, can be received only through faith (Rom. 5:2; Eph. 2:8–9). The writer of Hebrews calls on believers to emulate those who lived godly lives by faith (Hebrews 11).

[3] **Kingdom of God/heaven** – The sovereign rule of God. At the present time, the fallen, sinful world does not belong to the kingdom of God, since it does not submit to God's rule. Instead, God's kingdom can be found in heaven and among his people (Matt. 6:9–10; Luke 17:20–21). After Christ returns, however, the kingdoms of the world will become the kingdom of God (Rev. 11:15). Then all people will, either willingly or regretfully, acknowledge his sovereignty (Phil. 2:9–11). Even the natural world will be transformed to operate in perfect harmony with God (Rom. 8:19–23).

WEEK 12: SUMMARY AND CONCLUSION

We will conclude our study of Ecclesiastes by reviewing and summarizing the big picture of Ecclesiastes as a whole. Then we will consider a few questions for final reflection on *Gospel Glimpses*, *Whole-Bible Connections*, and *Theological Soundings*, all with a view to appreciating the book of Ecclesiastes in its entirety.

The Big Picture of Ecclesiastes

The refrain "all is vanity" is woven throughout Ecclesiastes. The Preacher poses seven problems of human life: the vanity of toil and human efforts (1:12–2:26), humanity's ignorance of the future (3:1–15), the presence of injustice in the world (3:16–22), the pursuit of wealth (5:9–19), unpunished wickedness (8:10–15), the common fate of humans (9:1–10), and the brevity of human life (11:7–12:7).

The Preacher emphasizes "all is vanity" so strongly that he has been supposed to be a teacher of unrelieved pessimism. However, in addition to and in spite of the sevenfold vanities highlighted above, the Preacher also recommends the pursuit of enjoyment (2:24; 3:12, 22; 5:17; 8:15; 9:7–9; 11:7–12:1). The theme of God's gifts occurs frequently in these passages. The opportunity to enjoy life is a gift given by God himself. This is the main reason the Preacher recommends the pursuit of pleasure: it is a gift from God.

The good things God has given us are intended for our enjoyment. To enjoy them is to do God's will. We must accept our ignorance of God's purposes and the reasons he has permitted evil to exist. Thus, for numerous reasons, we should take life as we find it and enjoy what we can. First, we cannot change the lots that God has chosen for us (2:26; 3:14, 22; 5:18; 9:9). Second, we cannot know what God has in store for us (3:11, 22; 8:14). Third, life is short and death inevitable (5:17; 9:9; 11:9; 12:1). These are incentives to enjoy all the more what God gives in the present. The recognition that toil is part of what God has allotted to us in this life, and that reliance on our own efforts is in vain, enables us to find enjoyment even in our toil.

▶ Gospel Glimpses

The meaninglessness that the Preacher so graphically describes and which fills him with such despair is a picture of living in this fallen world and without God. It is a foundational teaching of Genesis 1 and 2 that God created the world and called it "good." The Bible begins with God, the sovereign, good creator of all things: "In the beginning, God created the heavens and the earth" (Gen. 1:1). God's creative handiwork, from light to land to living creatures, is called "good" (Gen. 1:4, 10, 12, 18, 21, 25, 31).

Genesis 3 records the terrible day when humanity fell into sin and when *shalom* (peace) was violated. Humanity fell and was subjected to the curse of God. This brought into the world meaninglessness, vanity, and frustration. The rest of the Bible describes this frustration to which the world was subjected.

The Preacher is correct when he says a world that does not take God into account is meaningless. However, the New Testament tells us that the world is not just subject to endless cycles of meaninglessness. There is something new, in the person Jesus Christ. He has rescued us from the meaninglessness of the curse that plagues us.

Christ has rescued us from the vanity of the world by subjecting himself to that same vanity. He who is God chose to subject himself to the conditions of a world under covenant curse in order to rescue the world from the effects of that curse (Gal. 3:13).

The life of Christ may be seen as a record of moving from one situation of worldly vanity to another. He came into the world, but the world did not recognize him (John 1). His expectant mother could not find a place to rest in order to give birth. His life goes from one rejection to another, culminating in its last week as the people withdraw their support of him, his disciples desert him, Judas betrays him, and Peter denies him. But the ultimate experience of the world under covenant curse, the world of vanity, is when the Father departs from Jesus on the cross and he cries, "My God, my God, why have you forsaken me?" At this point Jesus dies, and he dies for a purpose—to rescue us from the effects of the curse.

Has Ecclesiastes brought new clarity to your understanding of the grace of God? If so, how?

Were there any particular passages or themes in Ecclesiastes that brought the gospel home to you in a fresh way?

Whole-Bible Connections

Jesus taught us to read the Bible with him in mind (Luke 24:44). Our search for eternal life, rest, joy, and justice moves us beyond creation's subjection to futility, to Christ (Rom. 8:20). The movement to Christ is not by direct statement but by the words of the "son of David" (Eccles. 1:1) that reveal the futility of everything that is not of God. Throughout Ecclesiastes, we are led to other answers, other solutions, and other wisdom than the world's vain promises of satisfaction, happiness, and fulfillment. Ecclesiastes forces us to yearn for and look to the one in whom true life is found. Our eyes are repeatedly taken heavenward for God's ultimate and eternal provision, of which Christ becomes the ultimate revelation (2 Cor. 4:6; Eph. 1:17). He is the world's supreme sage (Matt. 7:24–27), as well as the ultimate embodiment and demonstration of the "wisdom of God" (1 Cor. 1:24, 30; Col. 2:3).

How has this study of Ecclesiastes helped shape your understanding of the redemptive work of God throughout the biblical storyline?

Were there any themes emphasized in Ecclesiastes that helped you deepen your grasp of the Bible's unity?

Were there any biblical connections that you made through Ecclesiastes that you had not noticed before?

What connections between Ecclesiastes and the rest of the Old Testament were new to you?

What connections between Ecclesiastes and the New Testament were new to you?

Theological Soundings

Ecclesiastes contributes to Christian theology. Numerous doctrines and themes are clarified and reinforced throughout Ecclesiastes, such as God, providence, creation, the fall, and the sinfulness of humanity.

Has your theology been shaped or changed as you have studied Ecclesiastes? How so?

How does Ecclesiastes uniquely contribute to your understanding of God, creation, humanity, and Jesus?

What specifically does Ecclesiastes teach us about the human condition and our need of redemption?

What theological themes struck you the most in Ecclesiastes?

> ## Personal Implications

God inspired the book of Ecclesiastes to transform us. As you reflect on Ecclesiastes as a whole, what implications do you see for your life?

What implications for life flow from your reflections on the questions already asked in this week's study concerning Gospel Glimpses, Whole-Bible Connections, and Theological Soundings?

What have you learned in Ecclesiastes that might lead you to fear God, turn away from "vanity," and trust more firmly in his providential care for you?

As You Finish Studying Ecclesiastes . . .

We rejoice with you as you finish studying the book of Ecclesiastes! May this study become part of your Christian walk of faith, day-by-day and week-by-week throughout all your life. Now we would greatly encourage you to continue to study the Word of God on a week-by-week basis. To continue your study of the Bible, we would encourage you to consider other books in the *Knowing the Bible* series, and to visit www.knowingthebibleseries.org.

Lastly, take a moment again to look back through this book of Ecclesiastes, which you have studied during these recent weeks. Review again the notes that you have written, and the things that you have highlighted or underlined. Reflect again on the key themes that the Lord has been teaching you about himself and about his Word. May these things become a treasure for you throughout your life—this we pray in the name of the Father, and the Son, and the Holy Spirit. Amen.

KNOWING THE BIBLE STUDY GUIDE SERIES

Experience the *Grace* of God in the *Word* of God, Book by Book

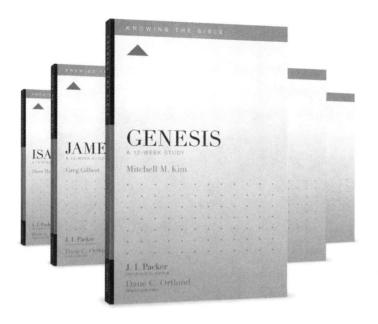

Series Volumes

- Genesis
- Exodus
- Leviticus
- Numbers
- Deuteronomy
- Joshua
- Judges
- Ruth and Esther
- 1–2 Samuel
- 1–2 Kings
- 1–2 Chronicles
- Ezra and Nehemiah
- Job
- Psalms
- Proverbs
- Ecclesiastes
- Song of Solomon

- Isaiah
- Jeremiah
- Lamentations, Habakkuk, and Zephaniah
- Ezekiel
- Daniel
- Hosea
- Joel, Amos, and Obadiah
- Jonah, Micah, and Nahum
- Haggai, Zechariah, and Malachi
- Matthew
- Mark
- Luke

- John
- Acts
- Romans
- 1 Corinthians
- 2 Corinthians
- Galatians
- Ephesians
- Philippians
- Colossians and Philemon
- 1–2 Thessalonians
- 1–2 Timothy and Titus
- Hebrews
- James
- 1–2 Peter and Jude
- 1–3 John
- Revelation

crossway.org/knowingthebible